D0353513

Rethinking Educational Leadership

Also available from Continuum

Personalizing Learning – John West-Burnham and Max Coates
Transforming Education for Every Child: A Practical Handbook – John West-Burnham and Max Coates
Schools and Communities – John West-Burnham, Maggie Farrar and George Otero
Spiritual and Moral Development in Schools – John West-Burnham and Vanessa Huws Jones
Understanding Systems Leadership – Pat Collarbone and John West-Burnham
Learn to Transform – David Crossley and Graham Corbyn
Education for Social Justice – John West-Burnham and Laura Chapman

Rethinking Educational Leadership

From Improvement to Transformation

John West-Burnham

continuum

Continuum International Publishing Group
The Tower Building   80 Maiden Lane, Suite 704
11 York Road   New York, NY 10038
SE1 7NX

www.continuumbooks.com

British Library Cataloguing-in-Publication Data
A catalogue record for this book is available from the British Library.

ISBN: 9781855396586 (paperback)

Library of Congress Cataloging-in-Publication Data
A catalog record for this book is available from the Library of Congress.

West-Burnham, John, 1946-
   Rethinking educational leadership : from improvement to transformation
/ John West-Burnham.
      p. cm.
   ISBN 978-1-85539-658-6 (pbk.)
   1. School management and organization. 2. Educational leadership. I.
Title.
   LB2805.W46 2009
   371.2–dc22

                                        2008048264

Typeset by YHT Ltd, London
Printed and bound in Great Britain by MPG Books Group Ltd

Contents

Preface

Like most people of my generation involved in education, the underpinning assumption guiding our thinking as practitioners, researchers and academics has been the prevailing orthodoxy of school improvement. Many individual careers have been the personal expression of the development of the theories of school improvement; reputations have been made and relationships built around a dominant and abiding hegemony. And it has worked – in many cases policies and strategies derived from the theory of school improvement did actually lead to schools and systems improving. School improvement theory has lasted for the simple reason that there has always been evidence available of its impact.

This book is written out of a sense of frustration with the inability of school improvement as a strategy to keep pace with the demands and challenges of the context in which schools have to work. In particular, there is the abiding issue in the English education system of reconciling excellence with equity. Although schools have, in many cases, improved out of all recognition, this could be seen as essentially a 'catching-up' exercise, i.e. the school is performing according to what would be expected given its social environment. A range of factors explains why a school is performing in the way that it is and our understanding of the variables that determine school success is growing all the time. In some ways this book can be seen as part of a series that covers my perception of the key issues facing school leaders in most education systems. This book could be seen as part of an informal series that began with *Personalizing Learning*, moved on to *Schools and Communities* and *Spiritual and Moral Development in Schools* and then on to *Understanding Systems Leadership* (all published by Network Continuum).

It will be clear from the references at the end of this book who my academic and intellectual sources and guides are. Equally important has been a range of people who in different ways, often unknown to them, have provided me with insight and inspiration, opportunities and endorsement: Geoff Barton, Sir Tim Brighouse, Tony Bush, Laura (Mole) Chapman, Hasan Chawdhry, Dame Pat Collarbone, Jane Creasy, Pam Curtis, Brent Davies, Katy Emmerson, Maggie Farrar, Richard Fawcett, Paddy Flood and all members of the Leadership Development Schools Project in Ireland, Tony Gelsthorpe, Jan Gispen, Tom Hesketh, Vanessa Huws Jones, Jill Ireson, Jeremy Kedian, Mark Lofthouse, Ian McKenzie, Paul Maclenaghan, John O'Neill, George Otero, Hazel Pulley, Maggie Roger, David Smith, Geoff Southworth, Ronald Stones, Ken Thompson, Richard Wallis, Tony Wells. To those who feel that they should be on this list and are not – my deep apologies.

As has been the case for several years, the production of this book would not have been possible without the skills, commitment and care of Ingrid Bradbury.

As is customary, I hereby exonerate them from any blame or guilt by association while gratefully acknowledging numerous acts of kindness and encouragement, conversations, examples and models, challenges, opportunities for collaboration, and countless insights and links.

This book is dedicated to Edmund and Carly—with love.

John West-Burnham

Introduction

Understanding leadership

This book is derived from two deep personal prejudices. First, just as germs eventually evolve to counteract even the most powerful antibiotic, so education systems are becoming immune to school improvement. This does not invalidate the strategy, far from it; there are still many situations in which it will work and for which it is appropriate – just as many antibiotics still work. However, in many contexts school improvement is just not working – working harder and with greater vigour do not seem to improve its limited efficacy given the profound changes in the context in which schools are operating. The relevance of school improvement may also be worth questioning when we are actively considering a future without schools *qua* schools.

The second prejudice is that perhaps we have been improving the wrong thing. At the most cynical level, it seems to have been the case that school improvement has worked best in contexts where the socio-economic factors have been positive. It does seem to be the case that the theory and practice of school improvement works best when the contextual factors are propitious. After two generations of policy initiatives, research and incredible professional commitment, there are still enormous problems in securing equity across most education systems. It does seem to be the case that the highest performing school systems are those with the lowest levels of child poverty and that academic success is directly linked to living in areas with high social capital. Certainly, in England, school improvement does not seem to have compensated in any way for the automatic advantages of high social class and the fact that the role of the family is significantly more important than the school in the primary years. It might be that we have been trying to improve the wrong thing – rather than improve schools we should have been trying to improve the family.

In some ways this debate is Mensheviks versus Bolsheviks; is the future about liberal reform or revolution? This is obviously an artificial polarity but it does beg the question as to how long some young people will have to wait in order to be guaranteed access to the same level and quality of educational provision as their peers across the system. Is it appropriate in a modern democracy to have a ten year strategy to take children out of poverty when a significant number of children has economic security as a birthright? This book is a reflection on the issue of moving from incremental improvement to transformational thinking, which is challenging in a number of ways.

The inherent conservatism of education systems perhaps explains the dominance of incremental improvement. It is not just the global context of schools that demands change – it is both the nature of schools themselves and the nature of the clients they serve that demands profound rethinking. If we are to transform children's lives then we need leadership that is transformational. Very few education systems in the world can be complacent about what they are achieving for their young people – for most systems there are issues of access, entitlement and equity. In all but a very few systems, equity is elusive and social justice remains as problematic as ever. Countries which are deeply committed to human rights and the rule of law seem to have no problem in operating an education system that institutionalizes privilege for the few and mediocrity for the many. This book explores what leadership for transformation might look like.

Rather than have a chapter that deals with well-understood basics (Leadership 101 perhaps) the rest of this introductory section is made up of a series of propositions about leadership that inform my thinking throughout the book. This is not to say that there will be absolute consistency, but rather that there is a range of 'taken for granted' assumptions that inform much of the discussion that follows. Some of these assertions are based on evidence, others are value judgements, some are clichés, some are derivative and others are highly contestable.

1 Leadership is primarily a moral activity; indeed the central component of any systematic definition of leadership would have to include the idea that the primary work of leaders is to translate principle into practice and to help create a shared and preferred future. In essence 'leaders do the right things', which presumes that they know what the right things are. Transformational leadership has to be morally driven leadership.

2 Leadership is the most significant of a range of complex variables that determines the success of schools. Many variables cannot be controlled directly; of those that can, leadership is easily the most controllable and the one with greatest potential impact and leverage. It is therefore essential to differentiate leadership from management and to recognize that, although they have to be in a symbiotic relationship, it is leadership that makes the difference.

3 Leadership works through direct and indirect influences – worryingly it is often the indirect ones that are the most compelling and significant. Leadership is about human interaction and perceptions and the nuances of influencing. Leadership only functions through human relationships.

4 Leadership cannot be taught, it has to be learned. Equally, leaders are not born; they develop and grow subject to the same range of variables that determine every other area of human activity that is grounded in learning.

5 Effective leadership is primarily determined by a range of human qualities that is reinforced by knowledge and behaviours. Leadership learning and development has to focus on those qualities and reinforcing them with knowledge so that leaders have the confidence to act.

6 Leadership is about the individual, although it is far more effective if seen as a collective capacity rather than personal status. This points to leadership being shared across the school and seen as a resource to be developed in an open way so that leadership is available where and when it is needed – there is no need to wait for permission.

7 Leadership in education is about learning: this means that the leader is a learner; the learning of others is the leader's primary concern.

The central theme of this book is the need to move from gradualist, incremental improvement to transformative strategies. Figure 1 (West-Burnham et al., 2007, page 20) shows the variables that influence the life chances of children and young people. In this model the school accounts for about 20 per cent of the factors that influence well-being and life chances, with the social and personal factors being far more significant than the school. It would therefore seem appropriate to question the energy and effort that goes into improving schools when it is the other variables that are more significant and have greater impact in terms of life chances and well-being rather than a narrow view of school performance.

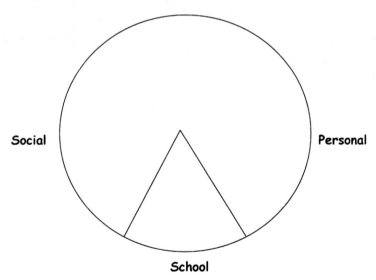

Figure 1 The variables influencing well-being and life chances

Figure 2 shows how schools have tended to be reactive and responsive to this situation – essentially looking to improve within a range of external constraints. In this context, schools are very much products of their environments – they are successful to the extent that the communities and families they serve are successful. In many social contexts the appropriate response to high levels of academic success and school effectiveness is 'this is as it should be'. There is little glory in ensuring that the advantages of wealth and social privilege are delivered. The real challenge is to be found in the measurement of added value – the extent to which disadvantage has been overcome. Schools are products of their geography, in the same way that the success of a lesson can be determined by the architecture of the classroom, so the effectiveness of a school will be, to a very significant extent, determined by its postcode. The issue, therefore, may be to spend time working on the implications of the geography before worrying about the architecture. Building a house on a flood plain places it in danger of flooding – no matter how well it is built.

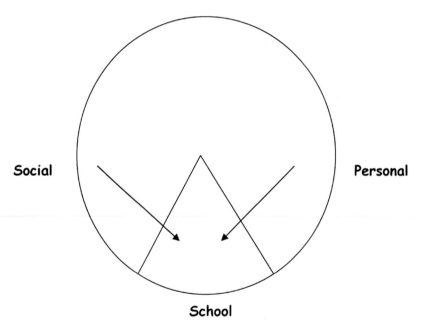

Figure 2 Schools as products of their context

Figure 3 shows the transformational approach that this book advocates – the school deliberately and systematically seeking to engage with the factors that make the real difference in terms of the nature and purpose of education.

The significant shift from Figure 2 to Figure 3 is the movement from reacting to

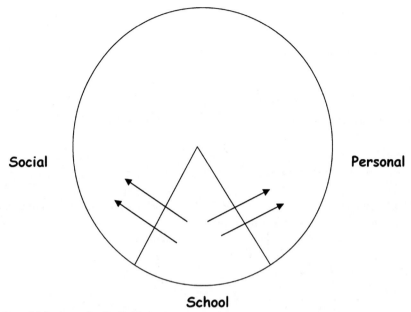

Figure 3 Schools transforming their contexts

anticipating, from coping to intervening, from 'find and fix' to 'predict and prevent'. Everybody knows that prevention is better than cure – the sad thing is that we do not always practise this in our personal and professional lives: it may not actually be seen as relevant or appropriate behaviour. Moving from a reactive culture to an inter-ventionist approach requires a fundamental rethinking of the nature and purpose of the role of leadership. It assumes a moral purpose, it requires innovation and crea-tivity, it needs courage as well as social skills – all qualities that will be explored in this book.

If leadership is a moral activity, then there is an imperative on leaders to work in a way that maximizes the possibility of what they believe in and aspire to being translated into the concrete experience of every child and young person. If the prevailing orthodoxy is not delivering effective education to every young person on an equitable basis, then the role of leadership has to be to question and challenge that orthodoxy. The more deeply embedded the orthodoxy the greater the need for transformational leaders. This implies leaders who:

- are committed to the need for and understand the implications of leadership for transformation;
- recognize the importance of creativity as a critical component of effective leadership;
- are deeply committed to providing a model of democratic leadership appropriate to educating future citizens;

- recognize that education can only function as a moral activity and therefore education leaders are moral leaders by definition;
- are confident and comfortable in their role working with and through people in an emotionally literate way;
- recognize that leadership is more than just a role and that it involves engagement with fundamental existential issues;
- are aware of the importance of intellectual perspectives in developing a personal rationale and strategy for transformation;
- are able to create and sustain learning communities;
- give high priority to their own growth, development and learning.

This list of qualities forms the basis for this book. Each chapter deals with a distinct topic and can be read as a free-standing article. However, the combination of all of the chapters forms an integrated approach to rethinking the nature of educational leadership.

1   Leadership for transformation

What is transformation?

Have no illusions, transformation is hard work. Witness the catalogue of failed New Year resolutions each year – apparently 22 January is the lowest emotional point of the year: it is when the Christmas credit card bill comes in and when it is finally conceded that the New Year resolution is not going to work. Most resolutions are about transformation (I will be healthier, more successful, nicer and so on); the cynical might argue that transformation is a hope and aspiration rather than a viable strategy. For some, educational transformation is an oxymoron, in the same way that sports personality, the adult male and British intellectual are oxymorons. By and large, education systems are not transformed; they emerge incrementally, often in a disjointed way – in fact disjointed incrementalism probably better describes more educational policy making than any other concept.

Transformation is a particularly persistent and evocative concept; it is one of those words that it is almost impossible to raise objections to. We seem to like the idea of transforming ourselves and the organizations that we work in. There are obviously very powerful religious connotations to the word – it alludes to rebirth, renewal and a new way of being. However, as is so often the case with such words, its power is often proportionate to the ambiguity with which it is used. Personal transformation is a highly complex notion and one that is fraught with difficulty. What exactly am I changing? At the same time, most adults will be aware of episodes in their life when there has been a fundamental reorientation: falling in love, marriage (or its modern equivalent), the birth of a child, or the loss of a partner. There are many other examples of significant changes in direction: giving up smoking, changing career direction, developing new skills and strategies and so on. But this can never be a 'taken for granted' process:

> If people were blank slates, it would be much easier to put new maps in place ... But people are not blank slates. Consequently, one of the first keys to effective change is recognising that people have existing mental maps, and they have them for a reason – they have worked and they continue to work well ... (Black and Gregersen, 2002, page 26)

Personal transformation might be seen as a process of redrawing personal mental maps, which is profound and challenging work. In some contexts it is probably not inappropriate to talk of damascene conversions. In other circumstances it might be more a matter of realignment. In many ways leadership development can be seen as reconfiguring mental maps – the movement from manager to leader is very much a matter of rethinking the maps and models that are used to make sense of the world. Sergiovanni (2005) talks of mindscapes rather than mental maps. For him mindscapes are:

> ... implicit mental frames through which reality ... and our place in this reality are envisioned. Mindscapes provide us with intellectual and psychological images of the real world and boundaries and parameters of rationality that help us to make sense of this world ... mindscapes are intellectual security blankets ... and road maps through an uncertain world ... (page 24)

Mindscapes 'are assumed to be true' (Sergiovanni, 2005, page 25) and are thus powerful determinants as to how we behave. I would suggest that it is our mindscapes that determine our engagement with the landscape; our mental maps determine how we construct reality and so inform the nature of our personal and professional journeys. Each leadership mindscape is unique, the product of all that makes us who we are. Effective leaders understand their mindscapes, work to systematically enrich and deepen them and use them to navigate their world. Cummings and Keen (2008) argue that a leadership landscape serves as:

- An atlas to help us understand the context we inhabit.
- A navigator to move from one situation to another.
- A 'prescencing device' to remind us where we are.
- A lens to help us understand perspectives and relationships.
- A balancing function to monitor the time spent in different landscapes. (page 14)

Leadership for transformation may require us to abandon long-used familiar maps and learn to use and create new maps. The *A to Z of London* is a wonderful map but it is for a very specific purpose. The London underground map is another map of London but it is presented in a totally different way – it is symbolic and it would be dangerous to use it to calculate distances or spatial relationships. The *A to Z* will not help you travel from Lincoln to London; it only has meaning and value in a given and limited context. There are numerous types of map serving the same geographical area – geological, meteorological, political and so on. The skill is in knowing both which map to use and how to read it.

Consider the concept of a zoo. The mental map of what constitutes appropriate accommodation for animals in captivity has changed out of all recognition over the past century. Zoos have changed in many significant ways: small cages of brick and iron have been replaced by more space, a more 'natural' environment, and programmes to ensure the survival of a species. However, some zoos have been transformed – the people are enclosed not the animals. It may be that with the development of information technology it will be possible to see animals in their natural state, in secure environments, rather than imprisoned in a totally artificial life.

Thus mental maps or mindscapes help us make sense of the world and explore alternative perceptions of it. If we share such maps, then shared social understanding and action becomes possible. Taylor (2004) adds to this modelling process by introducing the concept of the imaginary:

> ... my focus is on the way ordinary people 'imagine' their social surroundings, and this is often not expressed in theoretical terms, but is carried in images, stories, and legends ... the social imaginary ... is shared by large groups of people. ... [and] is that common understanding that makes possible common practices and a widely shared sense of legitimacy. (page 23)

Thus my personal mindscape or mental map could be a product of the prevailing social imaginary: the dominant hegemony. If I am a school leader and my professional mindscape is school improvement and I work in a system where the prevailing imaginary is one of incrementally improving schooling, then engaging in transformation will be very difficult – it is literally outside my personal mental framework; I cannot even envisage what it might look like. Hargreaves (2004) develops Taylor's model into the concept of educational imaginaries; in other words, the prevailing and dominant model of what constitutes appropriate and effective schooling. He draws a distinction between nineteenth and twenty-first century imaginaries and, in many ways, the transition from the one to the other could be seen as a process of transformation.

The process of leading transformation is very much the process of rethinking mind maps, mindscapes and imaginaries. Moving from a nineteenth century imaginary to a twenty-first century imaginary is essentially the process of leadership learning and development. In essence, the mindscape has to change in order to change the landscape; the private world has to be reoriented before the public world can be changed. This is the difference between extrinsic and intrinsic motivation, between imposed change and transformation that is sought and desired. The movement from a nineteenth century imaginary to a twenty-first century imaginary is a profoundly complex process in which personal values, professional judgements and personal histories are all called into question. Changing such beliefs and assumptions is very difficult and yet without a fundamental reorientation the potential for transformation will always be compromised:

> Educational systems are inherently conservative institutions, and that conservativism is in many ways justified. Still, just as educational systems eventually adapted to the agricultural and industrial revolutions, just as they eventually responded to the decline of established religion and the invention of print and audiovisual technologies, they will have to adapt as well to the facts of the globalized, knowledge-centred economy and society. (Gardner, 2006, page 225)

If personal transformation is difficult, then organizational transformation is even more challenging. In essence, the problems are multiplied in a geometric progression proportionate to the size of the organization and the complexity of its work. Authentic transformation in education is potentially extremely difficult if it is to move beyond the cosmetic. Transformation in education is so challenging, that sometimes the concept of transformation is compromised to suit what is possible in a given context. In the same way I can immediately become a healthy 62 year old by the simple expedient of redefining health. It is much easier to change the definition than to change the imaginary.

In the context of a discussion about transforming schools, three broad categories of usage might be identified: transformation as improved performance; transformation as the achievement of optimum effectiveness; and transformation as profound change.

Transformation as improved performance is most commonly expressed through the concept of transformational leadership. Bass and Avolio (1994, page 3) define it thus:

> Transformational leaders motivate others to do more than they originally intended and often more than they thought possible. They set more challenging expectations and typically achieve higher performances.

Transformational leaders achieve 'superior results' by focusing on the 'Four I's' – 'idealised influence, inspirational motivation, intellectual stimulation and individual consideration' (Bass and Avolio, 1994, page 3). The purpose of transformational leadership in this sense is to achieve improved results, higher productivity and better performance. In these terms transformation is about improvement, enhancing organizational capacity and maximizing effectiveness at personal and hence at organizational level. This is the most limited definition of transformation, focusing on the behaviour of leaders and using a range of strategies to improve the organization as it is currently conceptualized, in other words enhancing core processes – not questioning the integrity or validity of those processes. Applied to schools, this approach assumes that the school system is valid and appropriate, and only needs to be made to work better. This approach characterizes much of the work done in the 1980s and 1990s on raising standards in schools but using only a very limited definition of standards – literacy, numeracy and a narrow band of quantifiable outcomes. The entirely justifiable purpose of most reform initiatives centred on school improvement was to ensure that all schools achieved an optimum level of performance.

To use the concept of transformation to describe improved performance is to diminish and debase the term. It is a classic example of a usage that resorts to hyperbole at every opportunity; in A. J. Ayer's terms it becomes a 'hooray' word – it secures automatic approval. Improved performance is just that: a graduated, incremental movement of measurable outcomes. It is making the prevailing model more efficient. To claim it as transformational is to be reductionist and instrumental – to fall victim to the contemporary fashion that productivity is, of itself, virtuous. The best-selling book is not necessarily great literature. This first category is not transformation – it is improved performance.

The second category of transformation follows naturally from the first in that it describes an aspirational state when a significant proportion of schools has achieved a defined level of effectiveness– they are then deemed to have been transformed. For the DfES in England the purpose of leadership is to: 'contribute to the transformation of our secondary schools . . . ' (DfES, 2002, page 1).

There then follows a list of criteria which provides a powerful, aspirational, model focused on the achievement of pupils. Presumably a school will be deemed to be transformed when it can demonstrate that it meets such criteria as having:

- a core belief that *every* pupil can achieve high standards;
- effective systems that enable high expectations to be met;
- a strong contribution to improving the school system as a whole. (DfES, 2002, page 1)

Transformation in this sense is characterized by the school system, as a whole, becoming what it was intended to be. Change is therefore incremental and works within the prevailing model; it is about ensuring consistency of the first category across the system as a whole. Transformation becomes synonymous with optimum effectiveness across the whole system.

This approach is again beguiling but it compromises the potential power of the concept of transformation. There is no doubt that the various manifestations of the school effectiveness and school improvement movements made schools *qua* schools better. In terms of equity and social justice this was a vital process. However, it is rather akin to trying to improve the Banda copier to compete with PowerPoint presentations. (Younger readers may need to have this allusion explained to them.) If a train is going in the wrong direction it does not matter how punctual, reliable and comfortable it is – it will not get you where you need to go.

The third model of transformation moves beyond incremental improvements to the prevailing system and proposes a radically different approach in response to external rather than internal imperatives. According to Atwater and Atwater (1994, page 151)

> Incrementalist strategies apply when the organization's methods basically fit its current and predicted environment ... Radical transformational strategies are necessary when the organization is markedly out of fit with the demands of its environment ...

The first two approaches to transformation described above are essentially incrementalist; graduated approaches that do not question fundamental assumptions about the nature and purpose of the core business of the organization. It is, of course, a matter of fundamental judgement as to when an organization is 'out of fit'. Such a judgement may not be made on the basis of rational decision making; it will not necessarily be self-validating or self-legitimizing given the problems of:

- organizational inertia;
- conflicting stakeholder perceptions;
- high investment in the status quo;
- the lack of viable alternatives;
- the innate conservativism of many social processes.

O'Sullivan (1999, page 4) expresses the tension thus:

> When any cultural manifestation is at its zenith, the educational and learning tasks are uncontested and the culture is of one mind about what is ultimately important. There is, during these periods, a kind of optimism and verve that ours is the best of all possible worlds and we should continue what we are doing.

O'Sullivan goes on to distinguish between educational reform as working within the prevailing system and 'transformative criticism', which 'suggests a radical restructuring of the dominant culture and a fundamental rupture with the past' (page 5). For O'Sullivan there are three components to this process of 'transformative criticism': first, a critique of the prevailing orthodoxy; second, the generation of an alternative vision; and third, the demonstration of the process of change.

This perspective is reinforced by Taffinder (1998):

> ... transformation attacks both the current and the known world *and* the future. It is concerned with the creation of new opportunities, with the ability to junk conventional wisdom and destroy old (often cherished) advantages, to violate established business practice, compete in different ways, shut down competitors' angle of attack and behave in counterintuitive and, indeed, unpredictable ways. (page 36)

It is this emphasis on the counterintuitive and the unpredictable that begins to help us identify the true nature of transformation. 'Junking conventional wisdom' is one of the most powerful manifestations of transformative thinking – it is the junking rather than the enhancing of conventional wisdom that really begins to mark out the transformative approach. Taffinder goes on to make the point that 'more is invested in the past than in the future' (page 36) – in many ways transformation is about reversing that relationship. Hock (1999) reinforces this point:

> The most difficult part is to understand and get beyond the origin and nature of our current concepts of organizations; to set them aside in order to make space for new and different thoughts. Every mind is a room filled with archaic furniture. It must be moved about or cleared away before anything new can enter. This means ruthless confrontation of the many things we know that are no longer so. (page 7)

Taffinder and Hock are arguing for much more than strategies to boost performance or achieve optimum organizational effectiveness. Both are describing what Kuhn (1970) categorizes as a change in world view – the creation of a new paradigm:

> ... normal science ultimately leads only to the recognition of anomalies and crises. And these are terminated, not by deliberation and interpretation, but by a relatively unstructured event like the gestalt switch. (page 122)

According to the Kuhnian model, the history of scientific discovery is a series of gestalt switches that leads to the creation of new paradigms which in turn change the conceptual framework, language, methodology and epistemologies of the scientific community. Such a change also leads to a radical shift in the way in which questions are asked, the nature to the questions that are asked and the type of answer that is sought. The works of Galileo, Newton, Darwin and Einstein are so significant because they did not seek to improve and extend existing theories – they changed the fundamental assumptions. Evolution was available as a conceptual framework long before Darwin published the *Origin of Species* but it was a 'goal-directed process'

(Kuhn, 1970, page 171) designed to explicate a theological view of the world. 'The *Origin of Species* recognized no goal set wither by God or nature' (Kuhn, 1970, page 172). In this sense such ideas can be said to be transformational.

For Hock (1999, page 7) fundamental reconceptualization of the organization involves 'purpose, principles, people, concept, structure and practice'. For Taffinder (1998, pages 42–44) such a transformation has five characteristics:

1 It is comprehensive and requires an integrated set of solutions.

2 Transformation may require a challenge to the fundamental purpose of the organization.

3 Transformation may mean radical performance improvement.

4 Transformation requires solutions unique to the institution.

5 A necessary condition of transformation is dramatic change in the organization and in the individuals who make up its collective entity.

Hock and Taffinder both point to transformation as involving a fundamental reconceptualization: the creation of a new paradigm which questions every assumption, draws new conceptual maps and interrogates all structures and processes. Thus of the three models of transformation that were introduced at the start of this section, only the third is actually transformative – the first two are pseudo-transformations: incremental improvement. This relationship can be further explored through the following models.

Figure 1.1 demonstrates levels of change, distinguishing between shallow, deep and profound change. Shallow change is concerned with short-term outcomes and related improvement, and it is beguiling. It is rather like gardening, rearranging the flower beds, reshaping the pathways and putting in some decking. There is the superficial appearance of change but in fact it is cosmetic and short term and will need constant reworking (as government policies demonstrate). The garden is a better place – but only on the surface. A gardening culture allows us to believe that we are engaging in important work when all we in fact are doing is maintaining the status quo. There may be circumstances where this is perceived, properly, to be the real work of leaders but, as will be argued later, it is very difficult to be confident that any education system has reached a 'steady state' where all that is required is the nurturing and maintenance of the existing system.

Moving into deep change is much more challenging and demanding – working on the farm is much harder than working in the garden. However, the techniques are essentially the same as for gardening – to make things grow. The scale may change and the technology may be very different but the fundamental assumptions are the same. It is only when change becomes profound, when fundamental issues are being addressed, when the bedrock is being worked on that real transformation becomes a possibility. Obviously the deeper the change the harder the work; equally obvious,

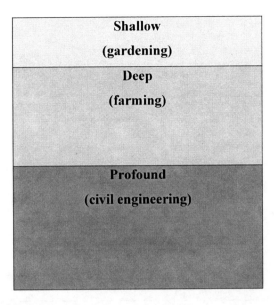

| Shallow (gardening) |
| Deep (farming) |
| Profound (civil engineering) |

Figure 1.1 Levels of change

the techniques and strategies that worked in the garden will not work for the civil engineering project. Governments and schools have become very adept gardeners; the need is for fundamental reconstruction.

Another way of picturing this process is to make use of Charles Handy's (1994) classic model of the sigmoid curve. In its original, elegantly simple form, it demonstrates how organizations and individuals wax and wane. Figure 1.2 offers an alternative interpretation.

At point A, organizations have three options. First, they can break out of historical and organizational imperatives and re-create themselves, so following the alpha track. Alternatively, they might engage in some improvement strategies and sustain their position on the beta track, or they can engage in cosmetic improvement that will only serve to delay their decline on the gamma track.

The crucial issue about point A is the extent that the school system recognizes that the context in which it is operating is changing. The greater the awareness of the major trends informing society, the greater is the likelihood of there being the fundamental reappraisal of the nature of the school systems and so the decision to follow the alpha track. Schools that choose to follow the beta and gamma tracks will be working in the old paradigm – the educational equivalent of believing that the sun circles the Earth, that mankind is the lowest order of angels and that the Earth is flat.

One of the great debates in archaeology is when the first city was established. Claims have been made for sites in Chile and India, with dates varying from 5,000 to

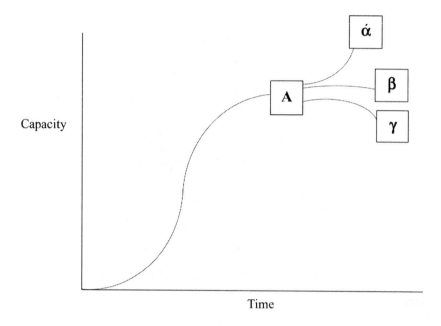

Figure 1.2 Organizational change and transformation

10,000 years ago. What is significant is the switch from nomadic to settled societies, from simple to complex communities, from pastoral and agricultural economies to trade, legal and financial systems. Whenever it took place, this transition was known as the 'great divide' – it was a point A, a period of social transformation which changed every aspect of human life and, crucially, this change was discontinuous, there were no precedents for it. Urbanization was a fundamental shift in human history, as was industrialization and the onset of the communication revolution.

Another way of understanding point A is by reference to Gladwell's (2000) notion of the tipping point. He uses the concept to explain changes in fashion, in crime rates and the behaviour of epidemics. He argues that tipping points have three characteristics:

> ... one, contagiousness; two, the fact that little causes can have big effects; and three, that change happens not gradually but at one dramatic moment ... (page 9)

It might be that education is approaching a tipping point in which numerous little causes might lead to the big effect of the transformation of the education system. One final example of the profundity of the change that transformation involves:

We cannot restructure a structure that is splintered at its roots. Adding wings to caterpillars does not create butterflies – it creates awkward and dysfunctional caterpillars. Butterflies are created through transformation. (Marshall, 1995, page 1)

The purpose of a caterpillar is not to be a better caterpillar – it is to become a butterfly. Perhaps school systems have been too busy improving the caterpillar and have forgotten what the butterfly looks like. Indeed one of the themes of this book is that there has been too much focus on improving caterpillars and not enough on the transformation needed to become butterflies.

Transformation is not about improving output or efficiency; it is not about incremental improvement or optimizing organizational effectiveness. Transformation is rather about the profound change of every component of the organization following a fundamental reconceptualization of its purpose and nature. Transformation is a process that ensures that an organization is appropriate to the context in which it operates.

Why transform?

There is a danger that transformation is seen as a self-legitimating activity. The 'buzz' of change is valid in its own right and the excitement of innovation will brook no opposition. There is no doubt that transformation can be emotionally exhilarating and intellectually exciting but at the same time there has to be a deep and rigorous justification to avoid the accusation of 'change for change's sake' and to secure commitment through consensus and engagement rather than control and compliance. There are numerous formulations as to why education should change; it is the extent of the change that is contested. However, this option may not be available to us:

I discern two legitimate reasons for undertaking new educational practices. The first reason is that current practices are not actually working … The second reason is that conditions in the world are changing significantly. Consequent on these changes, certain goals, capacities, and practices might no longer be indicated, *or even come to be seen as counterproductive*. (Gardner, 2006, page 10, emphasis added)

For some, the following list points to the need for radical rethinking; to others the need to maintain the current approach just because times are so challenging and change is so complex and rapid it is better to wait until it slows down or, better still, goes away:

1 The commitment and dedication that has been invested in school improvement for the past generation has not led to consistent and comprehensive improvement across the system. If anything, the continued focus on school improvement is leading to diminishing returns – we are getting less for more.

2 The growth in our understanding of how learning takes place points to a fundamental reappraisal of how the learning process is managed. In particular, there is a need to move from high confidence in the teaching of a subject or an age range to high confidence in enabling the learning of children and young people.

3 The concept of a curriculum is in need of radical overhaul, moving from information to be transmitted and replicated to knowledge to be created and re-created in response to continual growth in our understanding. To view the curriculum as the subject content that was defined by the Clarendon Commission in the 1860s is clearly absurd.

4 The implications of information technology which point to the learner deciding what is learned, where it is learned, how it is learned and assessed and when it is learned. Literacy may have to be redefined – texting, Facebook and so on may be the new expressions of literacy.

5 The social experiences of young people are very different to the lives lived by their parents: there seems to be less moral clarity and consensus; less focus on the community and more on the individual and different models of friendship and relationships.

6 Globalization and changes in the world economic order point to an increasingly small and interdependent world with small causes having massive effects.

7 The nature of work has changed and will continue to change with shifts in the balance of skilled/ unskilled, manufacturing/service, manual/knowledge based.

8 Politics has changed to almost total disengagement at local level, disillusionment at national level, with an increasing hegemony in terms of policy (it doesn't matter who you vote for, the government always gets in) and possible despair at international level with the Cold War being replaced by random terrorism.

9 And all of the above are taking place in the context of global warming – however caused.

There are numerous interpretations possible of the above factors, their relative significance and, crucially, how they might interact. Even the most conservative response to them would seem to point to the position that the status quo is really not an option.

Schools as caterpillars

The central proposition of this study is that schools are increasingly ill-matched to the society that they serve and will have to serve. Many have become efficient and effective caterpillars but have lost sight of their core purpose and are operating in an environment that is increasingly hostile to them. And yet, in their day, schools were the product of a profound transformation; they offered guaranteed access to free education, they educated a mass workforce, and they opened opportunities to many who had been historically deprived. The problem is that this was achieved by making schools microcosms of the world they served:

> In ... country after country, social inventors, believing the factory to be the most advanced and efficient agency for production, tried to embody its principles in other organisations as well. Schools ... took on many of the characteristics of the factory – its division of labour, its hierarchical structure and its metallic impersonality. (Toffler, 1981, page 45)

Gardner (1999) reinforces this view:

> ... apart from a few relatively superficial changes, human beings miraculously transported from 1900 would recognize much of what goes on in today's classrooms ... With the possible exception of the church, few institutions have changed as little in fundamental ways as those charged with the formal education of the next generation. (page 41)

The reason why the transformation of the education system is so vital is that schools are manifestations of the industrial age in an information society – they are increasingly dysfunctional and potentially irrelevant. They occupy the nineteenth century imaginary described by Hargreaves (2004). Schools are preparing young people for the world inhabited by their parents and teachers – not the world they will have to create and inhabit. It would be wrong to dismiss schools as totally negative forces; they have changed the lives of many for the good, they have provided stability, safety and hope, but often in spite of, rather than because of, the system. It is the integrity of individual teachers and the informal aspects of school life that often have the greatest impact – not the system of itself. The problem with schools is perhaps best exemplified in the concept of the extra-curricular – the social, the creative, the challenging and the exciting are marginal to the core business. The full logic of schooling or the nineteenth century imaginary is explored in Table 1.1.

Table 1.1 Assumptions underpinning schooling

1	Intelligence is measurable and fixed.
2	Learning can be measured through the replication of information.
3	Learning is chronologically determined.
4	Knowledge is made up of objective facts.
5	Knowledge can be divided into autonomous subjects that have the status of a canon.
6	Competition and individual performance are the most powerful motivators.
7	Prior learning and learning outside the school are marginal.
8	All people learn in the same way.
9	Time and space must be uniformly regulated.
10	The disciplines of life in school are a preparation for adult life.

These assumptions have led to a system of schooling that is remarkably pervasive and, by its own logic, successful. Schooling is, in virtually every respect, a product of the key imperatives of the nineteenth century – industrialization and urbanization.

> It needs to be acknowledged, then, that the model of the primary and secondary schools which came into existence with an education which was universal and compulsory is not only an outgrowth of industrialization but that it adopted the industrial pattern and applied it to learning. The underlying model for its organization was also bureaucratic ... (Beare, 2001, page 31)

The school system is, in many ways, a living fossil, unchanging in a world that has changed profoundly and irrevocably. One of the dominant characteristics of bureaucratic systems is that they are internally self-legitimating. The coelacanth survived because it had minimal interaction with its environment, but in doing so it became marginal and irrelevant to other life systems – it is a curiosity, a freak. As has been discussed previously, the context in which schools operate has changed so profoundly that the schooling system is faced with a stark choice. Either schools can be justified irrespective of changes in the societies they serve, in other words they have achieved the status of a platonic absolute: or they have to be radically and profoundly transformed so that they are engaged with the reality of the society they serve.

> ... the people who succeed at our meritocratic tests are empowered by our social hierarchies ... Over time these people, through their decisions and actions, tend to reproduce the institutions and procedures, including the testing procedures, that empowered them, thus putting more of exactly the same kind of people into positions of influence.
> ... The rest of us, those of us who don't excel at IQ-like tests or thrive in hyper

complex environments, are left behind. And some of the people left behind probably have mental abilities critical to our survival. (Homer-Dixon, 2000, pages 219, 220)

Education as a butterfly

If the arguments put so far are accepted, then it becomes necessary to explore the implications of transforming the school system. In one sense this is a futile activity as genuine transformation will develop a momentum of its own and it is impossible to prescribe in advance where such a process might go. A key theme of this book is how to create the leadership potential to enable the transformation process to occur. However, on the basis of the critique in the previous section, it might be helpful to explore alternative scenarios. A useful starting point might be to offer alternative assumptions to those set out in Table 1.2, focusing on education rather than schooling.

Table 1.2 Assumptions underpinning education

1	Intelligence can change and grow; it is multi-faceted and has to be measured using a range of techniques.
2	Cognitive development in the early years is pivotal to all subsequent learning.
3	The family and community are more significant variables than the school.
4	Learning has to be measured through the demonstration of understanding.
5	Every individual learns at a different rate; learning is non-sequential.
6	Knowledge is created through relationships.
7	Subject knowledge is less significant than cognitive and emotional development.
8	Profound learning requires intrinsic motivation and collaborative approaches.
9	Most learning takes place outside the school.
10	Every individual has a unique permutation of learning styles.
11	When and where learning takes place must be decided by the learner.
12	Full engagement in the community is the best preparation for adult life.

A powerful alternative perspective to prevailing orthodoxies is provided by the OECD study *What Schools for the Future?* (OECD, 2001). The study offers three main categories of possible future scenarios:

1 attempting to maintain the status quo;

2 re-schooling;

3 de-schooling.

In the first scenario the prevailing model of schooling is sustained and continues to be characterized by bureaucratic systems and centrally imposed uniformity, and the focus is on the individual school. The curriculum is centrally specified and accountability is results-focused. However, this scenario is compromised by a potential 'meltdown' in teacher supply caused by large-scale retirement, the difficulty of recruiting teachers in certain subject specialisms and in certain geographical areas, and the relative attractiveness of other professions.

The second scenario is characterized by two possible ways forward. In the first, schools become 'core social centres' with a high commitment to community engagement and integration with other services. In the second model schools become genuine 'learning organizations', in other words they are designed around the related notions of knowledge creation and the science of learning.

In the third scenario, de-schooling, schools are replaced by a multitude of learning networks making extensive use of information communication technology (ICT). An alternative to this scenario is the 'extension of the market model', which sees diversification of provision with a multiplicity of providers.

This very limited summary (based on Istance, 2002) does not do justice to the rigour of the original analysis. However, it is important to stress that the three scenarios, each with two models, do not represent alternatives. What is already happening is the emergence of permutations of the six. What is also important is that some factors, such as teacher shortages and changes in government funding, may force pragmatic change that might be hostile to morally driven transformation.

Transformation has to be a morally driven process, it has to start with clarity of purpose, and only then, according to Hock (1999, page 7), do principles, people, concept, structure and practice apply. On this basis and in the light of the discussion so far, it is possible to offer a number of propositions that might inform the debate about the nature of transformation in education:

1 The primary purpose of education is to develop the learning capacity of every individual.

2 Education is provided through personalized learning programmes which are negotiated on the basis of learning dispositions and needs.

3 The curriculum is defined by the learner as his or her total learning experience: cognitive, social, spiritual, moral, artistic and academic.

4 Schools are community learning resources; their primary purpose is to support and enrich learning in the family and community.

5 Schools work in federal relationships to serve a community, and are primarily accountable to the community.

6 Students progress through the system according to aptitude and need.

7 Education services are integrated with health, social services, housing and the police service.

8 Mentoring is the dominant learning strategy.

9 Teachers coordinate and support learning; information and assessment are managed through ICT. Schools are networked learning communities.

10 Members of the community are in schools as learners and supporters of learning.

11 Education is vertically integrated with nursery, primary, secondary, further and higher education being provided across the community.

12 Assessment and accreditation are based on portfolios of achievement.

There is a very real danger that transformational strategies are either seen as self-legitimating or that they are carried along on a wave of innovatory enthusiasm and to question them is to struggle against the stream and get swept away. Advocating transformation inevitably involves questioning and eventually rejecting long-established patterns and practices. And in education this means the personal life histories and the professional beliefs of educators – in advocating transformation we also advocate abandonment.

In the 1830s, the fastest way to get a message across the American prairies was by Pony Express. The company used the fastest horses and the best, and lightest, riders (ideally 13 year old orphans). But there was a limit to its capacity to improve the service. Horses can only run so fast, riders can only be so light. Communication across the prairies was not improved by doing more of the same, only by being better. It was transformed by the electronic telegraph and railroad. Improvement is finite, eventually even schools have to transform.

2

Leadership and creativity

You need chaos in your soul to give birth to a dancing star. (Nietzsche)

The things we fear most in organizations – fluctuations, disturbances, imbalances – are the primary sources of creativity. (Margaret Wheatley)

Creativity requires the courage to let go of certainty. (Erich Fromm)

You can never solve a problem on the level on which it was created. (Albert Einstein)

The above quotations point to a fundamental and disturbing truth: if leadership is going to even remotely address the issues identified in Chapter 1 then, for many, high degrees of anxiety and discomfort are involved. The movement from the efficient implementation of policies with carefully defined boundaries at school level to exploring radical alternatives for which there is no 'permission' or precedent is enormous. It is the courage of the artist displaying a new work that directly contradicts the prevailing canon and challenges the dominant orthodoxy. Improvement implies a gradual transition; transformation is about complexity, chaos and letting go of certainty.

The fundamental changes in the world economic order, best characterized as globalization, and radical changes in the perceived nature of society have led to an increasing recognition that reliance on historical patterns of leadership may be increasingly irrelevant. It is no longer possible to assume the status quo in social, economic, community, artistic or educational leadership.

Until the late 1980s, government education policy in many countries tended to be disjointed, incremental, *laissez-faire*, generic and enabling. Since then, policy has become increasingly interventionist, specific and prescriptive. However, it may now be possible to detect an emerging trend in which formal prescription is being paralleled by more enabling approaches. This might well be an implicit recognition that there is a limit as to how far a particular paradigm can be sustained and generate improvement. It also raises the possibility of moving from a rational/legalistic model of policy making to one involving creative and innovative approaches. There is a growing recognition that the role of government in both the private and public sectors has to create a climate of innovation in order to allow effective responses to increasingly complex problems. The economic liberalization of China is a classic example.

Leadership is often perceived as a 'higher order' activity, hence leadership is about 'doing the right things', management about 'doing things right'. Critiques of leadership in schools often centre on the preoccupation of leaders with the operational rather than the strategic. Leadership is equally often defined in terms of a responsibility for moral issues, setting organizational purpose and securing engagement and commitment of staff. It is clear that in most contexts where leadership is seen as significant it has a substantial impact on the organizational culture, structures and relationships. This chapter explores the idea that a defining characteristic of leadership might be a responsibility for creativity and innovation or enabling creativity and innovation in others.

The writers, artists and musicians working in Florence in the late fourteenth and early fifteenth centuries had no idea that they were part of what is now known as the Renaissance. But through networks, shared knowledge and influence they individually and jointly created a climate that allowed a new creativity to flourish. Florence in the fifteenth century was a mass of contradictory imperatives: full of tensions between the old and new orders, Church and state, and the intellectual, artistic and mercantile communities. It could be argued that it was this ferment of ideas that created the Renaissance: the tensions and the complexity, combined with the networks, provided both the stimulus and the means to bring about profound and fundamental change – in very many ways the Renaissance can be seen as intellectually, socially and artistically transformative. If you consider any of the great paintings of the Renaissance then it is immediately clear just how radically and profoundly different they are to their predecessors. In every crucial respect, technique, presentation and subject matter, they represent a fundamental realignment of what it means to paint. The change was in the nature of creativity and its expressions.

It should be possible to develop parallel models and examples for any sphere of human activity. The Italian Renaissance was largely focused on ideas and the pictorial arts. Music had a later renaissance; literature later still. The challenge would seem to be to develop strategies, policies, protocols and procedures that would enable both the letting go of the nineteenth century educational imaginary and the adoption of a twenty-first century educational imaginary.

Is creativity needed in leadership?

In one sense it could be argued that leadership and creativity are axiomatic; especially if transformational change is seen as the primary moral purpose of leadership. It may be a crude parody but a useful debating point, to argue that management is in many ways the antithesis of change and that 'managing change' is another great oxymoron. Leadership that is focused on incremental improvement is moving in the right direction but is always vulnerable to the myth that transformation is an extreme form of improvement, rather than a radical alternative. There is a range of arguments supporting the proposition that central to our understanding of leadership should be the idea of creativity:

- Leaders should model creativity in order to create a culture that enables a focus on creativity in all aspects of organizational life.
- Creativity is needed to translate generic, national, policies into appropriate and practical institutional and community strategies.
- The challenges of reconciling equity and excellence and achieving social justice require innovative approaches to how society and communities are organized.
- The humanistic model of an educated person requires the development of the creative potential in all people.
- Responding to social, economic and technological change requires the willingness to rethink and reconceptualize conceptual frameworks and practice.
- Fundamental challenges, such as global warming, point to the need to educate a generation that is flexible, adaptive and comfortable with change.

In his study of creativity and educational leadership Sternberg (2005) argues that:

> Transformational leaders ... are more likely to pursue any of a number of options that defy conventional paradigms, such as redirection and reinitiation. They are crowd defiers. (page 360)

By contrast, transactional leaders (who might be characterized as managers) 'typically provide contingent rewards, specifying role and task requirements and rewarding desired performance' (page 360). A school culture, based on transactional approaches, is unlikely to foster let alone implement creative approaches. Consistency, control, contractual integrity and formalized relationships are the prized indicators in the transactional/managerial culture. It is not that they are risk averse; these people are risk deniers.

What is creativity?

As a starting point it might be helpful to distinguish between 'Big C' creativity and 'little c' creativity (Gardner, 2004). Big C creativity is used to describe the significant innovation, the breakthrough in thinking, the paradigm shift, the creation of new knowledge – the great work of art. This is the scientific thinking that wins a Nobel Prize, the work of art in the National Gallery, the piece of music or the novel that goes into the canon. By contrast, little c creativity is to do with problem solving, being able to find solutions; it is a cognitive strategy and a way of learning.

There is an obvious issue in this approach that might be described as cultural relativism – what constitutes a work of art, what is the boundary between Big C and small c thinking – is it just a subjective judgement? In other words, is there a hierarchy of creativity? It might be more helpful to argue that the relative significance of creative acts should be determined by context. For example, to be the first school in a whole system to abandon automatic cohort chronological progression (year groups) is a significant act of creativity involving substantial innovation, some risk and a very real ability to translate principle into practice.

If creativity is defined in a different way, in other words not reified but rather seen as an activity, then it becomes more available. Thus it might be more appropriate to define creativity in terms of:

- the use of imagination, insight and originality;
- the development of a different product, process or outcome;
- the addition of value to an existing product or process;
- the use of higher order skills, knowledge and qualities;
- the potential to make a difference, to improve, enhance or enrich.

Creativity might be seen as a balance of technique and inspiration, for example the skills of the artist or scientist with the insight to use them in a different way – Michelangelo's *David*, Beethoven's Third Symphony, Darwin's *Origin of Species*, Einstein's Theory of Relativity. However, it could be argued that these are examples from one end of the spectrum. In all of these cases there are examples of interpretation and development which are of themselves creative.

In the same way, it can be argued that there are other manifestations of creativity that lack global importance but are nevertheless significant. These might well be classified as leading change, innovation and entrepreneurship. There is no doubt that Leonardo was one of the great creative thinkers of history – he had the vision of the helicopter, although it was Sikorsky who actually made one fly. In a culture dominated by theories of high art (grand opera is more worthy than a Hollywood musical), there is the danger that creativity in the fine arts is accorded greater social value than the invention of the World Wide Web by Tim Berners-Lee.

So creativity in educational leadership can be expressed in a wide variety of ways; the opportunities for genuine Big C creativity are probably very limited in an area of such common human engagement as education – there are just too many educators in the world. Transformative thinking is relative and contextual, but in all cases it involves questioning the status quo and offering radical alternatives that go beyond the historical assumptions and comfortable orthodoxy.

What are the characteristics of creative people?

According to Sternberg (2005):

> An effective leader needs creative skills and attitudes to generate powerful ideas; analytical intelligence to determine whether they are good ideas; practical intelligence to implement the ideas effectively and to persuade others to listen to and follow the ideas; and wisdom to ensure that the ideas represent a common good ... (page 348)

There is a significant academic debate about the relationship between creativity and intelligence. It does seem that the most venerated creative geniuses were intelligent in the context of Gardner's theory of multiple intelligences, in other words high IQ is no guarantee of creativity and creative ability in one domain is not matched across all domains. Creativity is the optimum expression of one or more of the intelligences.

Gardner's colleague at Harvard, David Perkins, has developed the 'snowflake model of creativity': six elements, each complex in its own right and interacting in a highly complex way. According to Perkins (1981), the more of these psychological traits a person has the more creative he or she tends to be. The traits may be defined as:

1 The need to create meaning and order, to simplify, to structure and clarify that which is seemingly chaotic. Creative people have a high tolerance for complexity and ambiguity; they thrive on synthesizing and making sense.

2 The ability to identify problems and then understand the components of the problem, in other words asking the right questions and then exploring a wide range of options to find answers.

3 The skills and strategies to find new perspectives and different approaches. For example, thinking in opposites and contraries and challenging fundamental assumptions.

4 The willingness to take risks, seek challenges and an associated acceptance of the possibility of

failure. The ability to learn from failure as a means of pursuing personal boundaries and competency.

5 The willingness to be open to criticism, take feedback and test ideas against the perceptions of others.

6 Being intrinsically motivated; relishing challenge and deriving enjoyment from the work itself. Intrinsic motivation is about the joy and passion of the creative process – it is not about rewards, recognition or status.

These criteria can be applied to the great composer, the highly effective community leader, the visual artist or the technological innovator.

It is clear from the above six characteristics that creativity is as much an emotional as a cognitive process. It is a complex blend of knowledge, skills and technical (craft) ability with passion, commitment and 'stickability'. Another significant component, in an increasingly complex equation, is the possibility that creativity may be driven by a moral perspective. Sternberg argues that the defining characteristics of creative people are:

1 nonentrenchment – willingness to question

2 integration and intellectuality – taking a holistic view

3 aesthetic taste and imagination

4 decisional skill and flexibility

5 perspicacity – insight

6 drive for accomplishment

7 inquisitiveness

8 intuition. (Sternberg, 1990)

In addition to these higher order intellectual skills, personal qualities and intuitive behaviours it is worth reflecting on the need for what might be called 'craft skills', the ability to translate ideas and imagination into the tangible and understandable, in a form that can be engaged with by others. Thus the composer has to have the technical ability to orchestrate, the painter has to understand colour, the scientist to move from theory to application and production.

What are the characteristics of creative organizations?

Can a committee write a poem? The answer is probably 'Yes'. Although it might not be great poetry it would probably be recognizable as a poem. The experience of writing it would probably be a significant learning opportunity for those involved. And therein lies the clue. Simply creating time, space and opportunity, and taking creativity seriously is probably one of the most important routes to working in a school that is serious about its commitment to creativity. If the school's leadership creates a culture in which creativity is valued, then the school is more likely to foster creativity and the leadership, in turn, is more likely to be creative by virtue of working in a propitious and supportive environment. Such a culture would have the following (well-understood) characteristics:

1 shared values and core purpose;
2 open, rich and sophisticated communication;
3 high engagement and commitment;
4 intellectual diversity – a broad spectrum of ideas and interests;
5 high trust and autonomy;
6 opportunities for rich and diverse learning;
7 a culture of review and reflection, openness and de-privatized practice;
8 learning resources to support creative projects.

Once the culture has been established then protocols and best practice working are needed to help ensure consistency and equity of experience across the school. For example, the Philadelphia School of the Future uses the following structured approach to change and innovation:

The 6 I approach
Introspection: review of vision, experience of the change process, models of learning.
Investigation: research, benchmarking, identifying best practice.
Inclusion: developing collaborative relationships, bridging with the community.
Innovation: generating and testing solutions.
Implementation: putting projects into practice.
Insight: review, reflection, learning and planning the next phase.
Source: Microsoft Innovative Schools Project

This model provides a powerful example of a carefully worked through strategy which reconciles the need for systematic and analytical approaches with the need for innovation and does not neglect the centrality of inclusion and effective learning.

Kelley (2005) provides an interesting alternative perspective to enhancing innovation by focusing on the different types of individual required to enable innovation:

The Ten Faces of Innovation

The Learning Personas

Individuals and organizations need to constantly gather new sources of information in order to expand their knowledge and grow, so the first three personas are *learning roles*:

1 The Anthropologist brings new learning and insights into the organization by observing human behaviour and developing a deep understanding of how people interact physically and emotionally with products, services and spaces.

2 The Experimenter prototypes new ideas continuously, learning by a process of enlightened trial and error.

3 The Cross-Pollinator explores other industries and cultures, then translates those findings and revelations to fit the unique needs of your enterprise.

The Organizing Personas

The next three personas are *organizing roles*, played by individuals who are savvy about the often counterintuitive process of how organizations move ideas forward:

4 The Hurdler knows the path to innovation is strewn with obstacles and develops a knack for overcoming or outsmarting those roadblocks.

5 The Collaborator helps bring eclectic groups together, and often leads from the middle of the pack to create new combinations and multidisciplinary solutions.

6 The Director not only gathers together a talented cast and crew but also helps to spark their creative talents.

The Building Personas

The four remaining personas are *building roles* that apply insights from the learning roles and channel the empowerment from the organizing roles to make innovation happen:

7 The Experience Architect designs compelling experiences that go beyond mere functionality to connect at a deeper level with customers' latent or expressed needs.

8 The Set Designer creates a stage on which innovation team members can do their best work, transforming physical environments into powerful tools to influence behaviour and attitude.

9 The Caregiver builds on the metaphor of a health care professional to deliver customer care in a manner that goes beyond mere service.

10 The Storyteller builds both internal morale and external awareness through compelling narratives that communicate a fundamental human value or reinforce a specific cultural trait. (Kelley, 2005, pages 8–12)

It would be interesting to speculate (assuming that the model is transferable) on the extent to which Kelley's archetypes are available in schools. While aware of the dangers of stereotyping, one can see many collaborators, directors and caregivers and perhaps not so many experimenters, cross-pollinators and storytellers. Schools in general are woefully short of experienced architects and set designers in terms of the quality of learning experiences found consistently across the school.

Issues and implications

Much as I enjoy writing, I very much doubt that my next book will be a novel that would involve Big C creativity: that is just not me. But I do enjoy writing, so I have a form of creativity available to me. What can be done to help those who are not comfortable with the demands of creative thinking in the context of transformation? Is it possible to build bridges between creativity in the performing and visual arts and the leadership of organizations? I am not convinced that a day spent learning to throw a pot would actually advance the cause of the twenty-first century imaginary but then there is a joy and sense of liberation, possibly, in learning to drum or dance, which might be transferable.

Perhaps we need to understand the relationship between nature and nurture in the development of creativity, and explore models of learning and the development of strategies that will enable more people to see themselves as potentially creative. For example, there is a number of programmes available, based on models of brain-based learning, which seem remarkably successful in enabling people with no apparent 'natural' aptitude to become very accomplished with drawing.

Perhaps we need to spend more time investigating the relationship between inspiration and craft/skill in creativity. In other words worry less about Big C creativity and focus more on the practical skills and techniques and strategies that will build the confidence to engage in creative activities. And at the same time recognize the importance of the social preconditions for creativity to flourish, for example openness, tolerance, free speech, recognition and respect, support, acceptance of diversity and pluralism. All of this will only work if we move away from absolutism in creativity and recognize that creativity, like quality, is not an absolute – the principle is one of 'fitness for purpose', what works, what is right at this time, in this context.

In the final analysis it is a matter of how far can society sponsor, support, indulge and celebrate heretics, radicals or even lateral thinkers? What is clear is that transformation will not occur without them.

3 Leadership and democracy

Understanding democracy

The debate about the status and nature of democracy is akin to that about whether teachers are professionals. It is possible to develop criteria to demonstrate that teachers are, or are not, professional. The debate hinges on the relative significance attached to a range of criteria and is usually resolved by subjective judgement. One way of resolving what is an increasingly circular debate is to abandon the emphasis on status and focus instead on practice – professionalism rather than professional. So with democracy; rather than try to resolve the differences between competing claims, this discussion will focus on the consensus – prevalent in Europe – as to what democratic societies actually do. This is to move from a relativistic Platonic debate about democracy as a possible ideal to a more pragmatic approach. What is vital is that the process of debating the nature and significance of democracy is seen as a key element in the portfolio of ideas that school leaders concerned with transformation are able to draw on.

> When we ask about the relationship of a liberal education to citizenship, we are asking a question with a long history in the western philosophical tradition. We are drawing on Socrates' concept of 'the examined life', on Aristotle's notions of reflective citizenship, and above all on Greek and Roman Stoic notions of an education that is 'liberal' in that it liberates the mind from the bondage of habit and custom, producing people who can function with sensitivity and alertness as citizens of the whole world. This is what Seneca means by the cultivation of humanity.
> (Nussbaum, 1997, page 8)

Democracy is, of itself, a transformative process; 'cultivating humanity' could be seen as an overarching aspiration for all educationalists. Becoming an active and knowledgeable member of a democratic society is fundamental to most perceptions of the nature and purpose of education. Schools are potential gateways to active citizenship or disengagement from the political process. Chomsky (2000) outlines the challenge for schools:

> Any school that has to impose the teaching of democracy is already suspect. The less democratic schools are, the more they need to teach about democratic ideals. If schools were really democratic, in the sense of providing opportunities for children to experience democracy through practice, they wouldn't feel the need to indoctrinate them with platitudes about democracy. (page 27)

The following list of criteria for a democratic society needs to be seen as interdependent and in no particular order of priority. The emphasis is on a democratic *society* rather than the political system. However, it may be useful at this stage to offer a brief and limited typology of democracy as a political system to clarify the debate. The most common usages of democracy as a political system seem to cover the following broad definitions:

'Pure' democracy: a system where all citizens have a direct involvement in the political process. This has probably never existed – ancient Athens was a democracy only for free men; women and slaves had no right to participate. As an ideal pure democracy remains important – it allows us to form judgements about the extent to which any system, community or institution is close to democracy by judging the extent to which there is genuine participation by all citizens.

'Representative' democracy: this covers a wide range of practice – it is often referred to as 'Western' democracy and is based on the election of representatives to a legislature at regular prescribed intervals. Such representatives are not delegates; therefore, choice is restricted to choosing those who will exercise real choice. This distinction between representatives and delegates allows for the debate about the location of sovereignty – which is only located with the people at the time of an election, in other words we are a democracy for one day approximately every five years.

'Totalitarian' democracy: usually a one party state whereby elections regularly return one party to power. This is often facilitated by the lack of any opposition parties or the use of criminal and corrupt practices at elections. This is democracy only in a symbolic or marketing sense.

In the context of this discussion, democracy is more than the arrangements for the allocation of political power. A democratic society can be said to have the following characteristics:

1 High significance is attached to *individual freedom* and *personal liberties* guaranteed by the *rule of law*.

2 In their personal and political lives, individuals are able to make *choices* which directly inform political and social systems, with the *majority* will prevailing, but minority rights being respected.

3 There is optimum *participation* in political and social processes with appropriate levels of influence. *Representatives* selected through the political process are *answerable* and *accountable*.

4 Democratic systems are *open* with maximum access to information and the sharing of knowledge to allow informed *consent*.

5 A primary function of governments elected by a democratic society is to *protect* the safety, wellbeing and economic and social security of their citizens.

6 Democratic societies work to ensure that their members lead lives which allow opportunities for *personal growth*, creativity, artistic expression and social fulfilment.

The words in italics probably provide a basic vocabulary of democracy. Each word carries a complex web of meaning and interpretation, and will be conditioned by historical, cultural, social and economic imperatives. Hence there is a need to avoid summative judgements and to see democracy as a relativistic and formative concept rather than an absolute. The only caveat to this position is that the process has to be one of enhancement of the various factors rather than their erosion or limitation.

A democratic society is therefore one that seeks to enhance, consolidate and extend the six characteristics outlined above. A democratic society is one that is committed to change, growth and improvement in its institutions and systems. This is a key-defining characteristic in contradistinction to totalitarian regimes, which invariably seek to prevent change and development. The process of becoming a democratic society is the process of maximizing each of the six above elements, which are now considered in detail.

Individual freedom

For many this is the *sine qua non* of democracy. It is the most evocative claim of any struggle to achieve democracy. Freedoms have traditionally had both positive and negative expressions. The positive freedoms include freedom of speech, of assembly and of conscience. The negative freedoms include freedom from want, hunger, persecution and so on. Combine these two approaches and a challenging manifesto emerges of a portfolio of personal liberties, enshrined in a constitution and guaranteed through the rule of the law. Thus democracy includes not just the right to vote for a government but also the right to criticize that government and to propose alternatives to it – a point lost on most totalitarian democracies. However, such rights automatically entail the recognition of the rights of others to engage in the same process – and therein lays the great strength of democratic societies and their fundamental weakness. Monbiot (2003) captures this tension:

> Democracy is unattainable unless it is brokered by institutions, mandated by the people and made accountable to them, whose primary purpose is to prevent the strong from oppressing the weak and to prevent people of all stations from resolving their differences by means of violence. The collective noun for such institutions is government. So democratic government, of one kind or another, appears to be the least-worst system we can envisage. (page 41)

Whatever ethical authoritative source is clamed for individual freedoms and personal rights it does seem that only a democracy can safeguard them in practice.

Choice

Personal and collective choice is fundamental to a democratic society. I am not living in a democracy if I cannot choose which books to read, which movies to watch, how and what to worship, whom to associate with and so on. Equally I have to be able to choose which government will make choices on my behalf. But, again, I have to accept that my choices will eventually be circumscribed by the majority. There will always be a tension between the stated preferences of the majority and the views of experts; however:

> ... most political decisions are not simply decisions about how to do something. They are decisions about what to do, decisions that involve values, trade-offs, and choices about what kind of society people should live in. There is no reason to think that experts are better at making those decisions than the average voter. (Surowiecki, 2004, page 267)

It might be tempting to think the more choice the better the democracy – is a country with 14 political parties more democratic than the country with two? The issue is obviously qualitative rather than quantitative – it depends how real the options are, and how genuine and significant the alternatives are. There does seem to be a very high correlation between levels of civic engagement, for example voting and the perceived validity of the choice, the greater the hegemony between parties the lower the turn-out at elections. It could be that political consensus denies democratic vigour. The increasing technical complexity of modern societies has tended to produce deference to experts and a willingness to surrender certain fundamental choices in order to preserve perceived greater freedoms. A combination of apathy and deference has tended to infantilize citizens in many societies creating dependency on a government that knows best.

Participation

Participation refers to the extent to which the members of a democratic society are actually involved in the political process. In a 'pure' democracy presumably every citizen would be directly involved in every decision. The scale and complexity of modern states clearly militates against this. In such systems democracy is essentially 'diluted' into a process of electing representatives who are perceived to have a mandate to exercise choices on behalf of their constituents. Participation therefore becomes symbolic; voting is on generic issues over a long timescale except where the issue is deemed so significant that a referendum is required – however, these are often advisory.

Thus political representatives may become surrogates and, according to local political traditions, delegates or representatives. Either way they are invariably deemed to be accountable – directly through the ballot box and indirectly through being answerable to the same laws as every other citizen. The greater the level of participation, the greater the level of accountability – which is manifested in moral terms as well as legal requirements.

Openness

Access to information is fundamental to the informed consent that is central to any notion of a democratic society. The validity of consent is directly proportionate to the integrity of the information on which it is based. Thus most democratic societies will work to minimize the amount of data that has restricted access and work to make the functions of government as open as possible, subject to personal confidentiality and the needs of national and commercial security. Openness is not about access; it is about the right to publish and debate so as to encourage the debate that informs the giving of consent.

One significant trend of the twentieth century might be termed the paternalism of the professions. The dominance of the professional classes across society led to the culture of 'need to know' in medicine, national security, education and, increasingly, across a wide range of political processes. It is remarkable how, across Europe, there is such a wide spectrum as to what should be classified as secret or confidential. It might reflect the maturity, confidence or trust of the government and its agencies.

Protection

Democratic societies accept a responsibility for the safety and well-being of their citizens. Thus democratic societies ensure the provision of education, health care, housing and security, and ensure that there is appropriate provision for the vulnerable and disadvantaged members of society. In doing this they demonstrate that democracy is as much about the quality of life as about political processes.

Personal growth

Democracy is about the capacity to lead a full and rich life, in other words to give expression to every aspect of what it means to be human. A democratic society is enabling in that it creates the environment which allows individuals to be able to choose a life that is enriching and fulfilling for them. It recognizes that over and above social and economic security there is a need for personal creativity to be expressed in the widest possible ways. One of the signs of a healthy and effective democratic community is diversity in the arts and literature.

In his discussion of John Dewey's view of democracy, Boisvert (1998) summarizes Dewey's model, which argues that democratic life is:

> ... difficult and challenging. It is not an easy path. Democracy requires vigilance, effort, and experimentation. The experimental spirit is important in order that democracies may always modify the means enacted toward the realization of the ideal.
>
> ... A democracy should be judged by the way all of its citizens are able to develop their capacities and thus grow in effective freedom. It should be judged by the way it encourages individuality ... (pages 71–72)

For Dewey democracy is about the extent to which the individual can flourish in community and society but this is a reciprocal relationship – the growth of the individual is a direct expression of engagement in the community and society:

> What the argument for democracy implies is the best way to produce initiative and constructive power is to exercise it. Power, as well as interest, comes by use and practice ... The delicate and difficult task of developing character and good judgement in the young needs every stimulus and inspiration possible ... I think, that unless democratic habits and thought and action are part of the fibre of a people, political democracy is insecure. It cannot stand in isolation. It must be buttressed by the presence of democratic methods in all social relationships. (1933, pages 345–346)

For almost every person in a democratic society the single most important relationship, after family and community, is the educational process – those who seek to destroy democracy will often seek to control education first.

The role of education in a democratic society

The model of democracy proposed in the previous section is deeply rooted in literate and engaged citizens. Indeed, it could be argued that literacy is fundamental to a democratic society; however, it is literacy in a cultural sense as well as a technical skill related to reading and writing. Building on Dewey's model of democracy, Boisvert (1998) summarizes his core propositions for education:

1 A system of education in a democratic society must not only be open to all its citizens, but must make a concerted effort to succeed in well educating them. In practice, this means paying attention to the differing situations of children entering the educational system.

2 The educational system must help increase freedom as power to select and accomplish adequate life-projects. It must also foster the growth of individuality.

3 Democratic education must widen the scope of student interests. Understanding history, the sciences, painting, music and literature are the prerequisites to breaking down barriers between classes and establishing a context for wider shared interests.

4 Education in a democratic society must also inculcate the habits of taking account of others prior to making decisions ... Democratic practice is marked by taking others into account, by considerations of consequences and how they impact beyond their immediately perceived benefit for the agent. (pages 107–108)

Dewey draws a very clear distinction between education and schooling. Schooling does not, of itself, constitute the basis for the development of a democratic society. Schooling has to be seen as a necessary, although not sufficient, component of education. The prevailing imperative of schooling is largely economic and vocational rather than democratic. The tension between schooling and educating can be represented in Table 3.1.

Table 3.1 Schooling and educating

Schooling	Educating
Teaching	Learning
Information	Knowledge
Generic	Individual
Competencies	Qualities
Linear	Complex
Employability	Socialization

Source: adapted from West-Burnham et al., 2007, page 41

In this model, schooling is presented as being essentially reductionist, instrumental and limited. Most modern democracies talk of education but in fact focus on schooling and this is manifested in the daily experience of school students across the world.

Teaching and learning

It is only necessary to look in many classrooms to see that they are focused on the teacher and designed for listening rather than engaging in learning. Most schools (and school systems) have high confidence in what they teach (the curriculum) and how they teach it (the role of the teacher). The emphasis is on the delivery of the curriculum to a class – not on the learning of the individual. This is maintained most directly in the automatic chronological cohort progression found in most systems, the prescribed curriculum and increasingly prescribed models of teaching, the time-tabling process and the hierarchical organization of most schools.

Few schools are designed with learning as the *a priori* of the educational experience. In fact, few systems, let alone schools, have any shared public definition of learning as the basis for designing the educational experience.

Information and knowledge

The lack of a shared definition of learning inevitably leads to a focus on the replication of information rather than the creation of knowledge in school systems. This is most powerfully demonstrated in assessment systems which tend to focus on the presentation of 'right' answers which are derived from a curriculum presented by teachers. Even in higher education there are very few examples of assessment focused on the creation of knowledge. In many systems, preparation for living in a democracy has become a subject called citizenship to be taught, memorized, replicated and assessed rather than a process based on experiences allowing individuals to create their own knowledge, demonstrated through understanding.

Generic and individual

Although most systems claim to focus on the individual (and assessment generally does this) the experience of schooling is largely generic. The schooling system is based on cohort progression, the teaching of groups and limited choices usually offered within narrow confines – it is not even table d'hôte, let alone à la carte; it is the no-choice conference dinner. It is the Model T Ford: any colour, as long as it is black. Thus the preparation for exercising choice in a democratic society is to be told there is a choice – not to learn how to exercise it as an individual by building personal understanding.

The movement to personalization of the public services is a significant antidote to the long-established pattern of generic provision. In education it has the potential to enable students to choose:

- what they learn
- when they learn
- how they learn
- who they learn with.

It would be wrong to underestimate the impact on schooling of these simple propositions and, equally, the need to build capacity to enable such choices to be made. However, for the Department of Education and Skills (DfES) in England:

> To build a successful system of personalised learning, we must begin by acknowledging that giving every single child the chance to be the best they can be, whatever their talent or background, is not the betrayal of excellence, it is the fulfilment of it. Personalised learning means high quality teaching that is responsive to the different ways students achieve their best. There is a clear moral and educational case for pursuing this approach. A system that responds to individual pupils, by creating an education path that takes account of their needs, interests and aspirations, will not only generate excellence, it will also make a strong contribution to equity and social justice. (DfES, 2004, page 7)

Competencies and qualities

The concept of an educated person is complex and elusive; there can be no aspect of the education process that is not contestable. The imperative to mass education in democratic societies has tended to see a reductionist approach to the curriculum in order to: (1) allow for consistency and uniformity; and (2) facilitate measurement to support outcomes and performance-based models of accountability.

This has inevitably led to a focus on those aspects of schooling that can be measured – thus the emphasis is on the tangible, pragmatic and instrumental. The qualities of an educated person – a moral sense, an engagement with cultural issues, the ability to debate and question – are inevitably subordinated to those elements that are controllable. Schooling tends to operate on the lowest common denominator; schooling is a necessary but not sufficient component of education, although too often the two terms are seen as synonymous.

Linear and complex

Schooling is a linear process – this is manifested in many ways:

- chronological progression through the school system;
- the formal, structured nature of the timetable;
- the linear nature of the curriculum;
- schemes of work and lesson plans;
- the organization of many classrooms.

Education, by contrast, is highly complex – it can take place any time, anywhere. It is not bounded by a curriculum, a classroom or the presence of a teacher. The family, community and peer group may well have greater impact than the school. What is taught at school may not be understood until the learner is at work or in any one of numerous social situations. Education often takes place by chance, in a random and non-sequential way.

Employability and socialization

For many education systems, the fundamental purpose of schooling is to ensure a suitably qualified workforce. This is both a national imperative and a personal entitlement. However, the extent to which the schooling system actually creates young people who are equipped to start work is a strongly debated topic in many democratic countries.

Schooling systems grew up in Western-style democracies when the demand was for large numbers of compliant workers with a relatively low skill base to staff factories engaged in mass production. The world of work has changed in these countries and schools have failed to keep up.

It is the broad range of human qualities, rather than the narrow and limited view of specific skills, that are needed for employment in the modern world, coping with complexity, and living a full and rewarding life. Such qualities might include:

- emotional intelligence;
- a commitment to personal growth and learning;
- perseverance and optimism;
- the ability to live and work interdependently;
- a clear sense of personal values.

Of course, schooling does not preclude the development of such qualities but they are often incidental and marginalized by the limited view of the curriculum.

The danger of a technical and functionalist view of education is that it will create dependency and inhibit the development of those individual qualities that are fundamental to citizenship in a healthy and vibrant democracy.

Education leadership and democracy

There is an inevitable tension between prevailing models of leadership and the characteristics of democracy described previously. In essence, it has been argued that democracy is about optimizing choice and participation. Much of the discussion about leadership, by contrast, tends to focus on the individual – the idea of the hero leader, the credence that is still attached to the notion of the charismatic leader. The prevailing orthodoxy about leadership identifies a range of distinctive characteristics:

- Leadership is focused on one individual who occupies the most senior position in the hierarchy.
- Leaders are invested with symbolic status.
- Leaders are seen as having primary responsibility for the vision and values of their organization and the parallel process of securing commitment.
- In many school systems, leaders have a clear personal accountability for the performance of their schools.
- Leaders often have significant powers of patronage and control over resources.

These points are reinforced by the structure of many schools, which is usually in the form of hierarchy with levels of power and authority being determined by the principal/headteacher. The professional career structure of teachers in many educational systems works through a process of increasing proximity to power. This trend is reinforced by two further factors.

First, in many Western-style democracies leadership in general, and in education in particular, there remains an essentially masculine model with much of the language associated with leadership being expressed through mainly masculine metaphors. This is reinforced by the dominance of Anglo-Saxon perspectives on the nature of organizations, social relationships and value systems. Second, education, like many other aspects of society, has come to be dominated by notions of technocratic efficiency and performance. As Apple (1982) puts it:

> The strategic import of the logic of technical control in schools lies in its ability to integrate into one discourse what are often seen as competing ideological

movements, and, hence, to generate consent from each of them. The need for accountability and control by administrative managers, the real needs of teachers for something that is 'practical' to use with their students, the interest of the state in efficient production and cost savings, the concerns of parents for 'quality education' that 'works' (a concern that will be coded differently by different classes and class segments), industrial capital's own requirements for efficient production and so on, can be joined. (page 151)

The centralizing tendency of many governments has seen policy become increasingly concerned with practice, with higher levels of specificity and control. This has tended to reinforce the power of institutional leaders by compromising individual professional autonomy. In some systems there is a stubborn resistance to this trend but the received wisdom of school improvement equates the effectiveness of the school with the personal effectiveness of the principal/headteacher.

There is no doubt that one individual can have a substantial impact on the effectiveness and performance of a school, but at what cost? The greater the emphasis on the individual the greater the potential cost in terms of disempowerment, loss of capacity, limited sustainability and failure to optimize the full potential of the staff. As Lambert (1998) expresses it:

> When we equate the powerful concept of leadership with the behaviours of one person, we are limiting the achievement of broad-based participation by a community or a society. School leadership needs to be a broad concept that is separated from person, role, and a discrete set of individual behaviours. It needs to be embedded in the school community as a whole. Such a broadening of the concept of leadership suggests shared responsibility for a shared purpose of community. (page 5)

If leadership is perceived as the characteristics of one person, trait theory, then it will inevitably compromise growth. However, if leadership is perceived as one manifestation of the democratic process, it has to be seen as a collective capacity rather than personal status. Lambert (1998) defines it thus:

> The key notion in this definition is that leadership is about learning together, and constructing meaning and knowledge collectively and collaboratively. It involves opportunities to surface and mediate perceptions, values, beliefs, information, and assumptions through continuing conversations; to inquire about and generate ideas together; to seek to reflect upon and make sense of work in the light of shared beliefs and new information; and to create actions that grow out of these new understandings. Such is the core of leadership. (pages 5–6)

This definition places leadership as a democratic process rather than as an alternative to democracy. There is a danger of oversimplifying the debate to a continuum of dictatorship to democracy, but in schools the potential for one individual to exercise significant personal, and sometimes arbitrary, power is considerable. Lambert's notion of building leadership capacity requires a significant conceptual shift if leadership is to be a means of achieving and modelling democratic practice rather than an alternative to it.

Immature Personal power Hierarchy Low trust Dependency			**Mature** Shared authority Teams High trust Interdependency
Control	Delegation	Empowerment	Subsidiarity

Figure 3.1 Shared leadership

Figure 3.1 offers a model of shared leadership which seeks to demonstrate the relationship between the various factors that determine the nature of organizational relationships. The various elements can be defined thus:

Control – power and authority located with one person or a small group. Very limited participation and choice for the majority; relationships are essentially hierarchical with clear lines of command and formal answerability with sanctions: a dependency culture based on immature social relationships.

Delegation – a balance of the handing over of responsibility and authority. On the left-hand side of the continuum, responsibility will tend to outweigh authority. Relationships are hierarchical and bureaucratic with clear definitions of areas of responsibility.

Empowerment – the level of authority is sufficient or greater than is needed to do the job. Individuals are able to exercise choice and discretion in their work within the context of broad organizational imperatives which they have contributed to.

Subsidiarity – the concept of subsidiarity is probably best understood as a form of federation – high degrees of autonomy within an interdependent structure with significant levels of choice and decision making at local level.

This movement from left to right across the continuum is characterized by a growth in choice, participation, trust and shared authority; the movement from an immature controlling relationship, based in personal power, to a mature interdependent relationship in which leadership is shared. In Crick's (2002) terms:

> Civic republicanism, that is the democratic spirit of direct participation, can and should be firmly rooted in regions, localities, neighbourhoods; and all powers that can be devolved should be devolved. (page 119)

Subsidiarity is the basis on which all federal states operate and it is the underlying principle informing relationships within the European Union (EU). And, of course, this applies as much to pupils and students as it does to teachers and all who work in schools. The movement from control to subsidiarity needs to be a feature of the whole school in order to inform how teams and departments, and most importantly classrooms, operate.

Such an approach creates an authentically democratic school where participation and choice are increased in a valid and genuine way at every opportunity. For Heifetz (2003) this means:

> The most interesting leadership operates without anyone experiencing anything remotely similar to the experience of 'following' ... When mobilised, allies and friends become not followers but active participants – employees or citizens who themselves often lead in turn by taking responsibility for tackling tough challenges, often beyond expectations and often beyond their authority. They become part-ners. And when mobilised, opposition and fence-sitters become engaged with the issues, provoked to work through the problems of the loss, loyalty and competence embedded in the change they are challenged to make. (page 69)

The movement from immature to mature organizations, from control cultures to genuinely democratic institutions, may involve a 'power sacrifice'. It is an act of significant personal courage for a leader to deliberately seek to create the situation where personal power is replaced by shared authority and organizational roles; structures, policies and processes are changed to reinforce the change. It may well be that this leaves the traditional school leader in a complex and ambiguous situation where external accountability is unchanged but internal relationships are totally altered. The changes are demonstrated in Table 3.2.

Table 3.2 Educational leadership for democratic education

Old order	New order
Personal power	Shared authority
Hierarchy	Subsidiarity
Control	Choice
Direction	Development
Instruction	Dialogue
Transaction	Transformation
Individual status	Collective engagement

Learning to be a citizen

The dominant activity in most schooling systems is the delivery, memorization and replication of information. The dominant modes of teaching involve teacher control of what is taught, how it is taught, how it is organized and how it is assessed. There is thus very little of what takes place in schools and classrooms which models, in any way, the fundamental principles of democracy. This directly contradicts much of what we are coming to understand as the basic principles of effective learning. It is not enough to provide information about what democracy is – in order to build commitment to, and engagement with, democratic principles three key elements need to be in place:

1 the school and classroom need to model democratic principles in practice;
2 learning about democracy has to be experiential;
3 learning has to be rooted in individual understanding.

Democracy and citizenship are not subjects – they are ways of life. It would be impossible to develop scientific understanding without experimentation; skills in sport cannot be developed by lectures; and drama involves active engagement and activity. It is not necessary for schools to be democracies in order for them to foster democratic engagement. Democracy is always a qualified and relative concept. However, it is necessary for democracy to be perceived as a way of living which requires the application of knowledge, skills and personal qualities. Schools can work to be more democratic than they are by using democratic processes which provide valid experiences that enhance engagement and understanding.

The danger is that democracy becomes a subject to be taught rather than a way of life to be lived. Schooling largely operates as a vehicle for the delivery of a curriculum, largely through subjects. It is these subjects that form the basis for the structure of the school experience and are the only recognized outcomes in terms of assessment and accreditation. Chomsky (2000) identifies the tensions and problems in this approach:

> The best way to discover how a functioning democracy works is to practice it. Well, schools don't do that very well. A good measure of functioning democracy in schools and in society is the extent to which the theory approximates reality, and we know that in both schools and society there is a large gulf between the two. (page 28)

The debate about the place of democracy in education has to link to the increasingly sophisticated debate about the nature of learning in schools. Schooling tends to focus on what might be described as shallow learning – the memorization and replication of information in a process that is largely extrinsically motivated. This approach inevitably results in compliance and dependency – the very antithesis of democratic principles. Education, by contrast, will be more concerned with deep learning, the conversion of information into knowledge through a process of reflection, testing and application. Deep learning is about intrinsic motivation where individuals accept responsibility for their own learning and development.

Personal understanding is the key outcome of the learning process; it is the direct manifestation of the movement from generic information to personal knowledge. Knowledge is internalized information which enables and informs action. Thus I might read a book about how to drive a car, but it is only when I engage in the process of learning to drive that the information in the book becomes practical knowledge that informs my ability to drive.

The essential stages in moving from information to knowledge – from the generic instruction to the personal – can be summarized as:

- The presentation of relevant information through lectures, reading, etc.
- Modelling of that information through discussion, debate, exercises, simulations and experiments.
- Application of the emerging understanding into real-life situations in which theories and hypotheses are tested against experience.
- Feedback, review and reflection on the implications of the inaction between theory and practice.
- Support in improving practice, application in new contexts, building and extending confidence.

This progression is, of course, artificially linear and will vary from individual to individual but certain factors are common to all learning to make this process work:

- The development of a shared vocabulary that facilitates dialogue and so enhances understanding.
- Intrinsic motivation based on perceived relevance and significance.
- Support for the learning process based on mentoring and feedback.
- The identification of the qualities and skills that are needed to support the development of understanding.
- Opportunities to fail safely on the way to personally valid success.

Preskill et al. (2000) identify a range of qualities or dispositions which are necessary to effective dialogue and therefore model the essential attributes of democratic life:

⇒ Hospitality: inviting, engaging and welcoming
⇒ Participation: the expectation that all will contribute and become involved

⇛ Mindfulness:	sensitivity and awareness
⇛ Humility:	the recognition that no one individual can have a monopoly of truth or insight
⇛ Mutuality:	recognition and respect for others
⇛ Deliberation:	careful and deliberate thinking based on logic, analysis, and evidence
⇛ Appreciation:	recognition, acknowledgement, celebration and respect
⇛ Hope:	An optimistic and positive outlook
⇛ Autonomy:	Balancing the needs for individuals to retain their personal integrity while working interdependently.

These qualities and dispositions seem fundamental to any collaborative human enterprise; they are fundamental to a successful team, the effective classroom and any collaborative human activity. Crucially, they are the prerequisites for successful debate and dialogue and thus serve as models for the democratic process. These qualities and dispositions are underpinned by a range of skills and behaviours which needs to be explicitly defined and addressed. Such skills and behaviours might include:

- deep listening;
- giving feedback;
- summarizing and reviewing;
- building consensus, managing conflict;
- open and formative questioning;
- building on and enriching contributions;
- recognizing multiple perspectives;
- challenging and testing assumptions;
- reflection;
- securing consensus and agreement.

The combination of this list of qualities and skills could serve as the basis for any model of effective social relationships; it also serves as a model for effective learning as well as being fundamental to any democratic process. It is possible to argue that the qualities and skills for democracy are the same as those for social and learning relationships – they are symbiotic. The issue for schools, therefore, is to be less concerned with the information about democracy and citizenship, and more concerned with creating authentic personal understanding.

Authenticity is fundamental to any learning process that is concerned with personal values and beliefs. Young people are remarkably perceptive when presented with superficial or formulaic approaches to matters which they regard as highly significant in their own lives. They are quick to spot hypocrisy, double-standards and inconsistency. So the teaching of democracy and citizenship has to take place in the context of genuine and valid activities which reflect the integrity of the topics being discussed.

A summary of the key elements in this discussion so far will produce a list of criteria for the development of democratic practice in schools:

1 Democratic practice involves choice and participation underpinned by rights and accountabilities.

2 Effective learning involves movement from theory to practice, from the generic to the personal, from information to knowledge.

3 Engagement in democratic activity requires a range of qualities, dispositions, behaviours and skills.

4 To have impact, learning about democracy and citizenship has to be authentic, in other words valid, concrete and consistent.

These criteria can be applied to a wide range of activities in schools:

- The explicit development of the qualities and skills as part of a meta-cognitive strategy.
- The introduction of choice and negotiation into planning of lessons – focusing on how if not what.
- Teachers using activities which demonstrate and reinforce democratic practices – and making explicit links.
- Developing representative and consultative bodies which have authentic authority and accountability with genuine choices and the ability to enact decisions.

Building democratic capacity

Democracy is fragile. Every nation reserves the right to suspend democratic principles and processes in times of crisis or emergency. But democracy is also subject to incremental erosion through an increasing emphasis on technocratic expertise or administrative efficiency. It is therefore essential to ensure that democratic principles and processes are deeply embedded in the social fabric so that they come habituated and the shared reference point for political engagement. In this respect schools have a fundamental role to play in developing democratic capacity – the willingness to engage in and strengthen the democratic infrastructure.

The extent to which a school is actively engaged in building democratic capacity can be judged by its responses to the following questions:

1 To what extent do the school's vision, values and mission statement demonstrate an explicit commitment to democratic principles?

2 How far is there an open flow of information to allow for informed engagement?

3 Does the school actively support and encourage the 'great freedoms'?

4 Does the school demonstrate a commitment to the dignity and rights of individuals and minorities?

5 Do the organizational structures and processes of the school model, as appropriate, democratic principles?

6 Is there a clear commitment to the enhancement of the 'common good'?

7 Does the school encourage critical analysis, debate and challenges?

8 Is there genuine participation, sharing of authority and building of trust?

9 Does the school seek to share authority?

10 Are there genuine choices available?

In her significant and valuable study, *Learners as Leaders*, Patey (2004a) makes a number of important recommendations based on the initiatives in the schools she studies:

- Where students are **learners they are empowered,** so **they are trusted and freed up to take responsibility for their own learning and the learning environment.** Once freed to take responsibility, young people can develop leadership skills.

- Schools and colleges find that learners are at the centre of the community if the **climate and culture of the organisation** allows **students to be empowered and able to contribute to the leadership and direction** of the organisation.

- Where students have a **knowledge and understanding of how they learn effectively** ... this enhances their leadership role within the organisation.

- The schools and colleges, for which case studies appear in this *Think piece,* create a culture and climate that promote leadership opportunities for young people.

  - These chances are **open to all** not just the able, articulate or vocal.

  - The curriculum developments and initiatives **are integral to** what the school offers and not bolted on.

  - Some schools are appointing senior staff to promote leadership across the organisation.

- ... evidence was seen that showed that younger students and primary school children are able to develop leadership skills and take on responsibilities ... (page 25)

Patey makes a direct link between learning, leadership, culture and climate in schools as well as a vital component of preparation for adult life. What follows are practical examples of strategies in schools taken from Patey (2004a), The BT Schools Awareness Supplement in the *Guardian* (2004b) and the 2020 Vision Supplement of the *Times Educational Supplement* (TES, 2003). The various examples have been integrated to provide generic illustrations of the possibilities for democratic development and participation:

- Focus group students being actively involved in reviewing the quality and nature of teaching.
- Members of the school council playing a full and significant role in the selection and appointment of teachers and senior staff.
- The school council being democratically elected, given a budget to manage, and specific authority and responsibility for an aspect of the school's life, for example development of an environmental area, responsibility for the design, building and operation of a 'safe-quiet' area in the grounds.
- Developing specific conflict management, negotiation skills and strategies to manage anger and violence through peer mediation, for example changing prefects into counsellors.
- Using ICT to develop partnerships with schools in other countries, which are then integrated into a wide-range curriculum activity to focus on issues such as racism, xenophobia, persecution and intolerance in order to develop a global perspective on citizenship.
- The conversion of the traditional school council (token consultation, and debates on uniform, meals and discipline) into a student leadership team that parallels and engages with the school leadership team.
- Moving from spasmodic charity events to sustained relationships involving time, skills and engagement as well as money.
- Students having responsibility as ICT managers and mentors for staff and adult learners.
- Students qualifying as sports coaches and leading sports teams.
- The student leadership team being actively involved in school management processes, for example the annual curriculum review, departmental performance, cross-curricular issues and special projects and initiatives.
- Students manage a weekly newsletter, radio station and TV station, which act as sources of two-way communication and debate.
- Students engage in real research projects which are fed into the school's policy-making process. Students become researchers, engage in market surveys, run focus groups and are thus able to contribute an evidence-based, authoritative voice to the development of the school.
- Students are given opportunities (and the skills) in order to be able to negotiate with teachers:
  - the focus of an aspect of the curriculum;
  - alternative methods of learning and teaching;
  - methods of presentation and assessment;
  - strategies for review and evaluation.

The school leaders involved in many of these projects reported a wide range of positive outcomes:

- improved academic performance;
- high attendance levels;
- improved relationships, less bullying;
- greater commitment and involvement.

The strategies outlined above give lie to the idea that preparation for citizenship in a democratic society involves knowledge of political processes – rather it requires engagement in social relationships. This requires an explicit school philosophy about the role and status of learners in schools; the following statement is taken from the values statement of Kambrya College, Berwick, Victoria, Australia (www.kambryacollege.com):

Relationships

The human values we live by are as valid today as they will be in our students' futures. Treating others with the same rights and privileges, as we would wish for ourselves is timeless. What has changed and will continue to change is the modern context that human interaction takes place in and the pressures this places on human relationships. Technology has meant that we can now communicate and relate to people in many different ways. We can form relationships with people across the other side of the world without ever having any personal contact; we are a truly global society. If we look at the development in communications over the last twenty years and then peer twenty years ahead, the world of science fiction may give us our best glimpse as to what may exist. Living in a global society is both a challenge and an adventure, which our students need to prepare for.

The values and vision of Kambrya College are reflected in many of the practical examples outlined above. There does appear to be a very high correlation in all types of organization between levels of commitment and engagement and the explicit articulation of values which are known, shared and understood.

There are, of course, substantial constraints on schools making the movement from helping students understand the principles of democratic life to being democracies themselves. It may well be that schools will always be microcosms of the society and culture that they serve. However, there is an equally compelling argument that educationalists should not just be reactive to society but should also be actively committed to changing it – the idea of education as a key vehicle for the achievement of social justice and so transformation. If this line of argument is accepted then there is a range of possible developments for schools (that do not involve the libertarian perspective that worry so many educationalists) by which they can become active protagonists in the development of democratic communities.

Democracy in education: the European dimension

Education systems are one of the most explicit and direct manifestations of national cultures, identities and social and economic priorities. Indeed, almost every component of a school system is subject to a wide range of variations that reflect historical, cultural and economic priorities. Within Europe, education systems have so far been immune from the type of trans-European initiatives that have influenced political, economic, financial and legal systems and structures across the European Community. This discussion seeks to contribute to a debate about the aspects of education in Europe that are not specific to one system, and which may form the basis for a deeper discussion of issues that transcend national boundaries and school systems.

It is not the purpose of this think piece to speculate on the issues surrounding possible standardization or integration of education systems. The principle of subsidiarity clearly prevents such moves, with education being seen as a classic example of an area which should be the preserve of national systems. In every education system in a federal state education is one of the key areas that is invariably reserved to state rather than federal level. However, it could be argued that there is a number of superordinate issues which transcend national systems in that they reflect the historical, geographical, cultural, political, economic and ethical dimensions of what it means to be a European.

While subsidiarity does emphasize the importance of locating authority at the lowest appropriate level, it also implicitly recognizes that there are some issues which are properly the concern of transnational bodies. These are recognized as certain fundamental rights which are properly the domain of supranational bodies. It might be that there are generic aspects of the educational process which fall into this category. Thus the freedom of speech has wide acceptance as a human right but is subject to a number of significant variations at national level, for example the status of freedom of information in the USA and the UK.

The gradual emergence of the concept of Europe since 1945 has been in sharp contradistinction to the previous 150 years, which saw the dominance of nationalism and the creation of national identity and the nation state as the key political imperatives.

This did not really diminish recognition of economic and political interdependency and of a cultural and moral heritage that transcended national interests and preoccupations. It is in this latter area that it might be possible to find a degree of consensus as to the nature of what it means to be European, and so a component of education that can be identified as common to all systems and thus an appropriate area of concern for educational leaders.

Until the late eighteenth century, the internal boundaries of Europe were largely based on the language spoken rather than the political allegiance, with borders on maps being shown by dots rather than lines to reflect the permeability of national identities. The changes in travel and communication, made possible by cheap fare airlines and all forms of electronic messaging, promise a return to a Europe of dots rather than lines. (Much of the thinking in this book is a product of email and low cost airlines.)

A liberal consensual view of Europe would stress diversity and eclecticism as positive virtues and the thoughtful debates about the nature of Europe stress the accommodation of apparent contradictions. There is unity in diversity in many areas of common concern increasingly fostered by an awareness of the impact of globalization that paradoxically has forced a simultaneous awareness of wider and narrower horizons. The growth in the membership of the community has been paralleled with an increasing awareness of regional identity and aspirations. The growth in the membership of the community in 2004 makes it even more important to have a meaningful debate on the nature of a European identity and the role of education in fostering such an identity.

Central to this debate is the role of educational leadership. For the purpose of this discussion, leadership is perceived as a higher order activity that has as its primary concerns:

- the ethical principles of the educational process;
- the creation of education for the future;
- the integrity of human relationships.

Used in this sense, leadership has an overarching responsibility for matters which are concerned with fundamental educational principles as well as the responsibility for managing the implementation of national policies. Of course, this is an artificial dichotomy; leadership and management are two sides of the same coin but without the recognition of the higher order responsibilities of leadership management that can become instrumental, reductionist and pragmatic. There are multiple permutations of the nature and purpose of leadership. In the context of this debate, a number of propositions can be advanced: leadership is fundamentally concerned with:

- creating a shared sense of purpose;
- inspiring and enthusing;

- securing engagement with a shared vision;
- recognizing the emotional dimension of work;
- creating authentic relationships;
- securing motivation and sustained performance;
- ensuring the moral integrity of professional work.

This is to argue that leadership has responsibilities over and above institutional systems and national concerns. If this proposition is accepted, then it becomes necessary to argue for the specific components of the ethical principles that might inform a debate about the European, common, component of educational leadership. In one sense there is already a hegemony based on the Judaeo-Christian tradition that is shared by all current members of the EU.

Even secular states have legal systems, social mores and political expectations which are explicitly derived from this common source. These principles are largely reflected in the underpinning assumptions guiding the work of the European Community:

- the primacy of the rule of law;
- the centrality of democratic institutions;
- the right to freedoms of speech and association;
- the right to employment and economic security;
- the right to education.

These principles make a number of fundamental ethical assumptions that have historically been associated with the most basic questions about the nature and purpose of education in society. At the most fundamental level, this is a debate about equity and entitlement. It could be argued that the preoccupation of national education systems in the last two decades with standards and performance have diminished the capacity of educationalists to relate their work to the more fundamental issues of educating. All societies make choices between a limited range of options. The debate for educational leaders is both about what choices should be made and how they should be made. The transversal policies of the Union provide a focus on issues that are perceived to be implicit to educational activities:

- Promote equal opportunities between women and men.
- Promote equal opportunities for disabled persons.
- Contribute to the fight against racism and xenophobia.
- Promote social and economic cohesion.
- Promote ICT in education.
- Promote language learning and teaching.

It is difficult to envisage any national education system that would not implicitly and explicitly espouse and promote these policies, but they might do so from a national perspective. There might also be a case for arguing that there are some issues that transcend European issues, in other words those with global implications such as climate change, population growth, poverty, disease, starvation and international security. This is not to deny the very real issues in moving the debate about leadership out of specific cultural contexts. Leadership is a social construct informed by a wide range of situational variables. Both within and between systems there will be significant variation in terms of organizational maturity, models of accountability and the inherent security and success of the system.

The issue, therefore, is to find a common approach which is not dependent on an anodyne consensus but rather actively promotes a distinctively European perspective which is based on fundamental cultural norms. It might be possible to summarize such an approach in the concept of liberal humanism, a philosophy rooted in tolerance, mutual respect and an aspiration to work towards rationality and objectivity. It is perhaps worth noting in passing just how much of the current European intellectual tradition is a direct result of interaction with the Arabic tradition not least in ensuring the survival of the classics of the ancient world and introducing mathematical and scientific, notably medical, thinking.

This could lead to a consideration, by educational leaders, of shared values based on a common cultural heritage which might include such elements as:

- the shared inheritance of the ancient world, notably Rome and Greece;
- the fundamental influence of the Jewish and Christian traditions combined with awareness of the Arabic and Chinese traditions;
- creativity in the arts;
- invention and discovery in the sciences;
- the humanistic tradition;
- the tradition of exploration and entrepreneurship;
- the radical questioning of norms and beliefs;
- tolerance and acceptance of diversity.

Of course, for each of these, there is a negative corollary, and Europe has demonstrated its capacity for intolerance and exploitation more than most of the rest of the world. However, this list might serve as starting point for a debate that seeks to extend the current boundaries of educational leadership beyond organizational integrity and limited definitions of success to a discussion of the principles that should inform the creation of educational systems for the future. The great danger is that the future of education in Europe will be the result of short-term bureaucratic incrementalism rather than values-based strategic thinking. The creation of a model of European educational leadership may therefore be seen as a genuine educational process based on the creation of a shared understanding of a common cultural and intellectual inheritance rather than the promulgation of bureaucratic consistency. This would mean the development of a leadership 'curriculum' which is as much concerned with the development of cultural understanding as with the professional knowledge necessary to lead schools.

Possible strategies for the increased democratization of education might include:

- A much greater emphasis on shared leadership with a far more equitable distribution of authority across the school, less emphasis on hierarchical structures and much more focus on team-based approaches.
- Patterns of accountability which distribute responsibility and have a much broader range of outcomes than many systems have today.
- Greater community involvement in schools, so that governance is a community responsibility and includes genuine opportunities for designing and developing local provision.
- Increasing emphasis on the personalization of learning with genuine and valid choices being made available in response to ability, maturity and motivation.
- The use of ICT to enhance communication, information flow, dialogue and decision making.
- The development of educators of a superordinate commitment to democratic principles which are then used to inform their professional practice.
- The development of curriculum models that focus on educational outcomes rather than school performance, and give high priority to the knowledge, skills and qualities needed to be successful citizens in a modern democracy.
- The recognition that effective leadership is a collective capacity, irrespective of age, gender, ability, creed or race rather than personal status.

4 Moral leadership

The purpose of this chapter is to explore our understanding of the issues surrounding the concept of moral leadership. Moral leadership is a powerful and compelling notion and the phrase has gained significant currency and approval, for example Sergiovanni (1992) and Fullan (2003). This chapter seeks to move from exhortation to analysis, to try to enhance our awareness of what moral leadership actually involves and how it might be better understood.

Moral leadership is, rightly, often depicted as the challenge of converting principles into practice; the abstract into the concrete, the aspirational into the actual experience. In the final analysis both morality and leadership are about behaviours which grow out of complex decision-taking. Decisions imply choices and it is in the process of choosing between options that leadership will be most clearly manifested as a higher order activity. Indeed it could be argued that one of the most significant indicators of the transition from management to leadership, and one of the defining characteristics of school leadership, is the growth in the range and complexity of decisions that have to be taken.

It is, hopefully, highly improbable that any headteacher would be faced with all the following dilemmas at the same time but all of them are real:

1 A small but influential group on the governing body are exerting significant pressure to introduce streaming and revive the 'traditional' uniform of blazers and ties in order to 'raise standards'.

2 There is only one supply teacher available but he or she has no classroom control and does not engage in any way with the classes he or she covers.

3 The inherited underspend is now 15 per cent of the school's budget. The finance committee and bursar argue that this is prudent and a necessary contingency fund for a 'rainy day'. You feel that it has been raining hard for several years.

4 Because of your school's excellent record for pastoral care you are under enormous pressure to admit a number of disaffected pupils from other schools. Your colleague heads clearly see this as a professional obligation – your leadership team is totally opposed.

5 The school kitchen has to be self-financing: you discover the most profitable item is 'Magi Fizz', a cocktail of chemicals masquerading as a fruit drink which has been shown to have an adverse effect on children's behaviour and learning. The annual profits from 'Magi Fizz' are the equivalent of one kitchen worker.

6 The school council accept, in broad terms, the school's uniform policy. However, some members have pointed out that there is a clear moral ambiguity in that, of all the members of the school community, only the teachers do not have to wear a uniform. A recent discussion in a critical thinking class highlighted the problems inherent in 'do as I say' rather than 'do as I do'.

Most of the scenarios are morally ambiguous – there is no clear indication of breaking a law. The response to them is therefore a matter of judgement. But on what basis can such judgements be made? What sort of authority might be invoked to justify a decision? How might a specific decision be defended?

It could be argued that all social decisions are essentially value-judgements – their validity is determined by who makes the judgement. Any discussion of moral leadership must therefore centre on the clarification of the nature of what it is to be a moral person.

This chapter starts by exploring the relationship between the concepts of ethics, values and morals. There is then a discussion of the nature of education as a process. This is followed by a review of what moral leadership might be and then what might be the ethical foundations of ethical leadership. The chapter concludes with a brief discussion of the issues surrounding the development of moral leadership.

For the purposes of this discussion, it may be helpful to draw distinctions between ethics, values and morals. Ethics will be used as an all-embracing term to cover the various alternative 'grand theories' of human behaviour. This is the abstract or philosophical level of debate in which principles are established and validated; all of the world's great faiths offer an ethical system, as do the great philosophical models such as humanism or liberalism. Values are the expression of ethical systems for a particular time and place; for a community or individual. Thus a person might subscribe to the Christian ethical principles but will interpret these according to a range of cultural and personal imperatives. So, for some Christians, the somewhat contradictory teachings of the Bible about violence might be interpreted as absolute pacifism, the notion of the Just-war or the legitimation of revenge. All are justifiable within the broad ethical system – it is the creation of the personal construct that makes them values. Morals refer to the analysis of meta-systems and personal values in action. Thus even if the concept of the Just-war is accepted, there still has to be a judgement as to whether a particular conflict meets the criteria for vindication as a Just-war. At all stages of the process – from ethical system to personal values to moral debate and actual decision making – there will be debate, interpretation and the formulation of roles, precepts and codes. It might be helpful to see the ethical system as the roots of the leadership 'tree'; these roots come together in the trunk which can be seen as the expression of personal values which in turn are extended out into the world as branches. The deeper the roots the stronger is the trunk the more resilient are the branches in coping with the storms of everyday life in school.

This is an immensely complex set of relationships and yet it is central to the most elementary definitions of what it means to be human; indeed, it could be argued that we create, find or lose our essential humanity by the extent to which we can participate in this process. It may possible to reduce this complex process to three deceptively simple questions:

1 What are the principles by which we should live?
2 How do those principles become personally valid and meaningful?
3 How should we act on the basis of those principles?

These questions reveal one of the most significant issues in any debate about human behaviour – the difference between normative (or prescriptive) statements and analytical statements. Normative statements are definitive, self-validating and are corroborated by reference to a higher authority. Analytical statements are derived from a process of critical elucidation and are often empirical in nature, for example derived from observation and experience. Normative approaches to ethics tend to produce 'grand theories'; analytical approaches focus on understanding behaviour and principles the process of debate.

It is much easier to adopt a normative stance – the ethical framework, personal values and moral behaviour tend to be defined in an authoritative way and there is only limited discretion or ambiguity available. For many this is comforting and reassuring and a reflection of a natural order. For others, such an approach is an abdication of personal responsibility and a denial of the integrity of the individual. It may well also be a repudiation of the world in which we live. The world is increasingly in the 'grey zone'.

> We understand better that in conditions of extremity, there are rarely to be found comfortingly simple categories of good and evil, guilt and innocent. We know more about the choices and compromises faced by men and women in hard times, and we are no longer quick to judge those who accommodate themselves to impossible situations ... (Judt, 2001, page xiv)

It is this move from ethical absolution to relativism – from acceptance and application to questioning and application – that raises fundamental questions for educational leadership.

The type of questions that might be raised include:

- What is the source of authority in leadership: authoritarian or authoritative, coercive or consensual, rationalism or absolutism?
- Is moral authority derived from positional status as valid as personal authenticity?
- Is there a difference between the moral basis of the relationships between adults and adults, and between adults and children?

Education as a moral activity

If educational leadership is about more than managing successful schools, then a number of profound issues is raised. The most fundamental questions centre on the nature of the educational process: 'What does it mean to educate someone?' and 'How do we recognize an educated person?' These are profound questions that will shape our understanding of schools, the curriculum, the roles of teachers and students, and the nature of educational leadership. The issue is one of processes and outcomes: how do we design an educational system that is ethical both in the way it works and in what it produces?

For example, most schools operate Rules, Codes of Conduct and so on, which represent a moral hegemony and as such are unexceptional. Such rules and codes are often normative rather than analytical and are implemented through hierarchical authority and sanctions. Compliance is rewarded and, where interpretation is necessary, it is usually done by those in authority. Moral behaviour is thus defined and prescribed, there are sanctions and rewards and there is the assumption that the prevailing orthodoxy is right for all. This is clearly prescriptive and models an ethical system that does not recognize the issues raised by Judt. Thus a first major issue for educational leaders is not just what ethical principles should inform behaviour, but how and why such principles should be formulated and then how moral norms should be agreed. It is much easier to formulate ethical principles than it is to create a process which creates those principles by modelling them in action. This is reflected in the difference between *a priori* and *a posteriori* statements, in other words statements that are self-justifying or justifiable only on the basis of experience respectively. This is at the heart of what it means to be educated: the acceptance of information or the creation of personal knowledge.

The difference is that between teaching people to behave in a moral way, or helping them to develop ethical understanding which is translated into a personal value system and so informs, and constructs, moral behaviour. For an educational leader, there are many themes or issues that require this sort of processing:

- the nature of childhood;
- the concepts of social justice and entitlement;
- the related notions of equity and excellence;
- the potential tension between individual rights and public responsibilities;
- the significance attached to personal autonomy;
- the source of teachers' authority;
- the nature of the learning process;
- the purposes of education;
- the place of leadership in education.

For each of these themes, there are ethical perspectives which have to be clarified, codified into a personal value system and then applied in the day-to-day life of a school. Schools are moral communities – there is no aspect of school life that does not have an ethical antecedent – all decisions are based on personal value systems and the morality of the school is expressed through the daily concrete experiences of all its members. It is impossible to separate the educational process from ethical considerations as the decision to educate is, of itself, an ethical decision. It may be appropriate, and somewhat salutary, to consider the moral perspective of education in Finland, the highest performing education system in the world and one of the highest ranking in terms of the well-being of its young people:

> The high quality and performance of Finland's educational system cannot be divorced from the clarity, characteristics of, and broad consensus about the country's broader social vision . . . There is compelling clarity about and commitment to inclusive, equitable and innovative social values beyond as well as within the educational system. (Pont et al., 2008, page 80)

There might be a case for arguing that a clear hegemony which enables a critical consensus helps to explain the most effective education system in the world – in other words, social transformation proceeds educational transformation and the two are indivisible:

> No single part of the overall innovation can or should be extracted or transposed from this society wide example, since the components are mutually reinforcing parts of a complex system. It is hard to imagine how Finland's educational success could be achieved or maintained without reference to the nation's broader system of distinctive social values that more individualistic and inequitable societies may find it difficult to accept. (Pont et al., 2008, page 92)

Moral leadership

It follows from what has been written above that any discussion about the nature of education systems and schools is essentially a discussion about ethics. Given the significance that is attached to the role of leadership in schools, it follows that a significant component of the debate about leadership has to centre on its ethical components. However, this somewhat blunt assertion needs to be developed to clarify exactly why moral leadership is significant. In this context, moral leadership might be defined as:

> Leadership behaviour which is consistent with personal and organizational values which are in turn derived from a coherent ethical system.

Moral leadership is important for a complex range of interacting factors. First, as mentioned above, education is, of itself, an ethically based process. Decisions as to the nature of the educational process are ethical decisions and, given the incredibly complex range of options and variables available, it would seem appropriate to argue that educational leaders should be ethically literate: they should be able to lead and participate in debates about fundamental educational issues. For example, the debate about whether the core purpose of education should be liberal and humanistic or instrumental and reductionist is live and real in most Western educational systems.

Two real issues emerge for our understanding of leadership: first, that leaders should understand the issues in the debate, and second, they should feel confident in participating in the debate. This implies that moral leaders are people who

> ... rather than following money or fame alone, or choosing the path of least resistance when in conflict ... are thoughtful about the responsibilities and implications of their work. At best, they are concerned to act in a responsible fashion with respect towards their personal goals; their family, friends, peers and colleagues; their mission or sense of calling ... (Gardner et al., 2001, page 3)

The second issue is that teaching is, or aspires to be, a profession. There are multiple definitions of profession, professional and professionalism, but one key characteristic is that professionals' work is characterized by its ethical purpose. Thus, at least in principle, doctors and nurses are concerned with relieving suffering; judges and lawyers with the search of justice. If teaching is concerned with the education of society, then it surely follows that the leadership of teachers should be characterized as leadership of professionals and should therefore have an ethical dimension.

Schools are social communities and this gives rise to the third proposition about educational leadership. One of the defining characteristics of an effective community high in social capital is that there is a consensus about the values and norms by which it should live and that one of the functions of leadership is a community in the articulation of, and sustained engagement with, the values that facilitate social cohesion. Leadership of a community involves securing agreement as to what constitutes the moral consensus, interpreting that consensus to respond to new situations and ensuring that the prevailing hegemony works for all members of the community.

The fourth aspect of moral leadership relates to the culture of a school. Culture is most simply and perhaps best defined as 'the way we do things round here'. In essence, culture refers to the language, symbolism and behaviour of an organization. It is thus a powerful expression of, and reinforcing agent for, the moral purpose of the organization. It is in the symbolic role of leadership that there are the greatest opportunities to reinforce, extend and apply community values, and this is powerfully reflected in the language and rituals of many schools.

The final element to be considered in this section is the notion of the leader as model – the personification and embodiment of the values of the school or community. In many societies, one of the defining characteristics of leadership is the exemplification of what that society most values. This imposes an incredible burden on the individual and it may not be sustainable but in essence one of the justifications for having leaders is that they help us see how we should be. However, given the status and authority accorded to leaders, not least in schools, there does seem to be a justification for the expectation that the behaviour of leaders will model and exemplify the expectations of the community in the professional context if no other. This is not to argue that every leader should be a paragon, but rather that his or her actions should be seen to be ethically based, value driven and morally consistent. Gardner (2006, page 151) provides a powerful synthesis of this debate:

> . . . I asked the cellist Yo-Yo Ma what he considered to be good work in his role as a leading musical performer . . . [He] outlined three distinct obligations: (1) to perform the repertoire as excellently as possible; (2) to be able to work with other musicians . . . and develop the necessary common understandings and trust; (3) to pass on one's knowledge, skills, understanding and orientation to succeeding generations . . .

This clearly calls for a model of leadership which is of a different order of significance to the notions of effective management and successful headship or the limited definitions of leadership which only focus on improvement or instruction. We expect our doctors to understand the ethics underpinning their medical decisions; we expect our judges' decisions to be rooted in jurisprudence, not just the application of statute; so we should expect educational leaders to be firmly rooted in the ethics of education. However, this raises the complex and challenging question of what ethical framework.

One topic that encapsulates many of the themes discussed above is the notion of equity and social justice in education. From one perspective, educational leadership committed to equity and social justice would not accept such strategies as banding, setting and streaming, as these are seen as reinforcing and exacerbating existing social divisions. Equally, inclusion would be seen as an absolute imperative and moral duty and collaboration between schools in support of effective learning as transcending professional or territorial affiliations.

The ethics of education

It is beyond the remit of this discussion to attempt to prescribe what *should* be the ethical foundations of education or even to describe what *could* be the basis for such a judgement. Rather it is important to analyse the basis on which the alternatives are identified and the means by which an ethical theory is chosen and developed into personal values.

The range of options of ethical systems is essentially the history of humanity. Individual choice will be largely determined by a range of cultural imperatives – of which education is probably the most powerful after the family and community. Ethical principles evolve and change in response to a wide range of complex variables and, in a form of natural selection, develop into distinct species which thrive in specific environments. There is therefore a choice which is reflected in the notion of a pluralist society in which diversity of opinion is not only recognized but actually celebrated in those societies which allow such diversity.

For educational leaders in Anglophone countries, the choices are circumscribed by the overarching Judeo-Christian tradition and by the fact that they work in democracies in which most significant decisions about education are taken by governments, and there is therefore a perceived duty to implement such policy. However, a cultural tradition, no matter how persuasive, and a government's policy, no matter how large its majority, do not grant automatic ethical veracity. A number of tests is necessary, which might include the following:

1 To what extent does this ethical proposition meet the tests of logic and reason?

2 How far is the proposition consistent with our scientific knowledge?

3 What would happen if this proposition became a universal law?

4 What would be the impact of this proposition on existing codes, cultural norms and patterns of behaviour?

5 If I were to adopt this proposition, what changes would occur in my life and would they be acceptable to my family and friends, those whom I work with and to me?

6 To what extent is this proposition consistent with higher order ethical principles?

A range of educational issues can be subjected to these tests and produce some interesting responses. Selection and streaming, for example, might be justified on short-term, expedient grounds but have significant ethical implications in the broader scheme of things. Opposition to inclusion begs many significant ethical questions. Inevitably, in a complex society, responses will be couched with caveats and a hierarchy of significance may well be adopted the 'greatest happiness' argument. The danger is one of ethical relativism, adopting a stance because it is the least objectionable or because it comes closest to achieving consensus.

One of the reasons why we still debate the nature and purposes of education (and why we still need leadership in education) is that the simplistic quantitative or authoritative responses are not blindly accepted. If the 'right answer' exists and had been found, then education would be a non-contentious human activity. But it remains a key debate in every society – even totalitarian democracies. How then is the educational leader to choose? By what criteria are policies to be accepted, rejected or undermined? On what basis are decisions to be taken when there is a genuine choice (and there still are many real choices to be made)?

The answers lie, perhaps, in the concept of ethical authenticity which Taylor (1991) captures most powerfully:

> There is a certain way of being that is *my* way. I am called upon to live my life in this way, and not in imitation of anyone else's. But this gives a new importance to being true to myself. If I am not, I miss the point of my life; I miss what being human is for me.
>
> Being true to myself means being true to my own originality, and that is something only I can articulate and discover. In articulating it, I am also defining myself. (page 29)

The problems of the ethics of education are best resolved by authentic educationalists. The personal authenticity of those who lead the debate is the best guarantee that education will allow the development of the authenticity of all:

> What our situation seems to call for is a complex, multi-levelled struggle, intellectual, spiritual and political, in which the debates in the public arena interlink with those in a host of institutional settings, like hospitals and schools ... (Taylor, 1991, page 120)

What are the components of the 'complex, multi-levelled struggle' for individuals, institutions and the educational system as a whole? For individuals Gardner is very clear:

> ... the work we do as adults should take into account our responsibilities to five different spheres: to our own personal set of values; to other individuals around us ... to our profession/calling; to the institutions to which we belong and to the wider world – people whom we do not know, those who will live in the future, the health and survival of the planet. (Gardner, 2006, page 234)

The struggle is to relate principle to practice in a way that is consistent over time and across varied contexts and then to translate that from the personal (the micro) to the system (the macro).

The development of moral leadership

Moral leadership cannot be taught it is part of a process of personal development – an 'intellectual and spiritual' struggle – which moves towards personal authenticity, intuitive understanding and so to action based on a sophisticated model of personal meaning. What is both encouraging and exciting, yet worrying and frightening, is that this is the process of becoming totally human; there is no difference between moral leadership in education and being a moral person – a course in ethics does not make people ethical.

> ... a continuing integration is called for between professional skills and a person's sense of character. It takes a lifetime to achieve such an integration. The people we personally admire are the ones who can, figuratively, continue to look in the mirror *over time*, instead of becoming gradually degrading Dorian Gray portraits ... (Gardner et al., 2001, page 246)

There is a number of strategies that can help to enhance what might be termed moral confidence – the ability to respond to complex situations in an ethically consistent way. None of the strategies that follow are unique to the development of moral leadership – it is the focus they are given that makes them relevant:

1 Engagement with the meta-narratives; in other words, reading the ethical classics, which will include the texts of the great religions, many works of literature, as well as technical works on ethics, education and leadership. The purpose of such reading is to deepen awareness and understanding, to extend one's personal vocabulary and mental models, and to stimulate reflection to create a personally coherent moral mindscape.

2 Reflection-in-action is a crucial learning process in which an individual's conceptual map is used to analyse actual practice, so that both map and the practice are interrogated and revised and hence inform future actions.

3 Mentoring, critical friendship and caring relationships can be powerful facilitating and mediating processes to support the first two strategies. They might be provided by a more experienced leader, a person who is a skilled facilitator or by a peer who is experiencing the same situation.

4 Networking, formal or informal, is a further powerful strategy that facilitates exemplification, clarification, problem analysis, solution generation, advice and reassurance.

Moral confidence and ethically based leadership in education cannot be tested. However, the leader who is growing in moral confidence might be able to engage in the following debates with confidence and fluency. What are the concrete and specific manifestations of moral leadership in respect of:

- the debate about the nature and future shape of education?
- the creation of a professional ethos based on consent rather than compliance?
- the development of a clearly aligned moral consensus across schools and agencies?
- a morally based school culture engaging with and informing a wider community?
- distributed leadership offering alternative models of structures and relationships?
- issues related to inclusion, equity and social justice?

5   Interpersonal leadership

The transformation of education is going to require an enormous investment in the quality of interpersonal relationships. It is not overstating the case to say that system transformation is directly contingent on the transformation of personal relationships. It could be argued that emotional intelligence, leadership and learning are in such a symbiotic relationship that they are actually tautological. This chapter is posited on a number of assumptions:

1 Leadership behaviour is a primary determinant of the emotional climate of a school. (Inappropriate leadership styles can create 'toxic organizations'.)
2 Effective learning is significantly determined by social and emotional relationships.
3 Social and emotional skills are essential components of high social capital.
4 Education is a constructivist, relational process; everybody has to be consciously competent.
5 Organizational life is the product of individual perceptions derived from emotional and social engagement.
6 Interpersonal behaviour is the tangible expression of the moral foundations of the school.

It is impossible to learn without involving the full spectrum of emotions. As Caine and Caine (1997) express it:

> Throughout our lives, our brain/minds change in response to their engagement with others – so much so that individuals must always be seen to be integral parts of larger social systems. Indeed, part of our identity depends on establishing community and finding ways to belong. Learning, therefore, is profoundly influenced by the nature of the social relationships within which people find themselves. (pages 104–105)

There is increasing understanding of the role that the emotions play in learning: in essence we give greater attention to, and remember more easily, experiences that have emotional significance, and neurological processing is influenced, to a substantial extent, by the emotional context. Damasio (2003) observes:

> Educational systems might benefit from emphasizing unequivocal connections between current feelings and predicted future outcomes ... (page 247)

A key criterion for an effective learning environment would therefore seem to be an appropriate emotional climate. Such a climate is very substantially the result of appropriate leadership behaviour. Leaders need to model the appropriate behaviour, clarify and define it, and intervene in order to ensure that it becomes the norm. As Goleman (2002) argues:

> Quite simply, in any human group the leader has maximal power to sway everyone's emotions. (page 5)
>
> Whether an organization withers or flourishes depends to a remarkable extent on the leaders' effectiveness in this primal emotional dimension.
> The key, of course, to making primal leadership work to everyone's advantage lies in the leadership competencies of emotional intelligence: how leaders handle themselves and their relationships. (page 6)

This is leadership at its most basic and fundamental – hence Goleman's use of the term 'primal', it is that elemental. One way of defining leadership in this context is to postulate what it is not; it is clearly not management. Management in this context might be seen as the technical aspects of a task or role, which might be completed without reference to other people. For example, it would be possible to complete a school development plan, a timetable or review the teaching of a colleague in a technically *efficient* way. However, for each to become *effective*, active engagement with people is required. A key transitional phase in the movement from management to leadership is the recognition of the 'rationalistic fallacy', understanding that rational structures and systems do not necessarily secure engagement and commitment.

By its very nature, transformational change is an emotional process. Indeed the greater the level of transformation the greater the emotional implications – think of the emotional impact of personal transformations: marriage, the birth of a child, divorce and so on. As social beings we make enormous emotional investments in order to make things work. Capra (2002) makes the emotional significance of change very clear:

> During the change process some of the old structures may fall apart, but if the supportive climate and the feedback loops in the network of communications

persist, new and more meaningful structures are likely to emerge. When that happens, people often feel a sense of wonder and elation, and now the leader's role is to acknowledge these emotions and provide opportunities for celebration. (page 108)

If leadership is seen as moving people from compliance to commitment, from acceptance to active engagement and from task completion to transformational thinking, then emotional intelligence is the vital medium. It is impossible to conceptualize any model of leadership that does not have emotional intelligence as a key component.

Schools are profoundly complex organizations – and are becoming more so. The demands on schools, and the dynamically changing environment in which they have to operate, reinforce the importance of relationship-based leadership. If the world were linear, predictable and controllable then leading organizations would be relatively simple. However, the world is complex, dynamic and driven by unpredictable relationships. Such a context generates fear and excitement, anger and hope, stress and fulfilment, engagement and rejection: in other words, emotional responses. At the heart of our understanding of leadership has to be the fundamental proposition that every leadership action will generate emotional responses. The problem is that the same action may well generate contradictory responses, even within an apparently homogenous group. An early lesson of leadership development is that responses are derived from perceptions, which are, by definition, subjective manifestations of private processes. Such processes will be emotionally driven and will be the foundation of future relationships; leadership behaviour determines relationships and so learning.

For all of these reasons it is argued that central to any definitions of leadership is the concept of emotional intelligence. However this assertion begs three fundamental questions:

1 What is emotional intelligence and how can we recognize it?

2 Why is emotional intelligence important in educational leadership?

3 How can we develop and sustain emotional intelligence?

What is emotional intelligence?

There are numerous models and permutations of definitions available around the concepts of emotional intelligence, interpersonal intelligence and so on. Three of the most widely known are Goleman (1998) and (2006) and Stein and Book (2000). Their respective models can be summarized thus:

Goleman (1998)	Goleman (2006)	Stein and Book (2000)
Self-awareness	Primal empathy	Intrapersonal
Self-resolution	Attunement	Interpersonal
Motivation	Empathic accuracy	Adaptability
Empathy	Social cognition	Stress management
Social skills	Synchrony	General mood
	Self-presentation	
	Influence	
	Concern	

What these models have in common is the emphasis on two dimensions – the internal and the external – the understanding of self and the capacity to engage with others. Goleman's 2006 list is particularly strong on engagement with and understanding of others. At this stage it might be appropriate to offer an attempt at a synthesizing definition:

> Emotional intelligence is the authentic range of intuitive behaviours, derived from sophisticated self-awareness and understanding of others, which facilitate effective social engagement.

The specific behaviours that would be implicit to such a definition might include:

- empathy
- motivation
- effective communication
- emotional self-management
- authentic engagement with others
- building trust.

Central to this model is the notion of authenticity; in other words these are not skills to be acquired, they are behaviours, which are rooted in the essential integrity of the individual. Singer (1997) provides a powerful reinforcement of this:

> So maybe Aristotle was right: the more we practise virtue, for whatever reason, the more likely we are to become virtuous in an inner sense as well. (page 200)

This quotation establishes an important link – emotional intelligence is a moral issue as much as a means of efficient communication. The behaviours can be viewed as a pragmatic toolkit but, in reality, they are manifestations of a moral perspective. Therefore it is important to stress the importance of personal authenticity – where social behaviour is the genuine manifestation of a coherent personal philosophy.

Emotional intelligence is essentially about being human – it is the most direct and public demonstration of values in action. Working together is about awareness, sensitivity, generosity, respect and genuine reciprocity. Gardner (1995) expresses it thus:

> I have in mind here individuals who are exquisitely sensitive to the needs and interests of others, and/or individuals who are correlatively sensitive to their own personal configuration of talents, needs, aspirations and fears. (page 31)

The inscription on the temple of Apollo at Delphi, 'know thyself', might be extended to 'know thyself, know others, then act'.

Why is emotional intelligence important in educational leadership?

The answer to this question rests in our understanding of the nature of education and the nature of leadership. In essence it is possible to argue that what is now described as emotional intelligence has always been understood as one of the central characteristics of the educated person. The ability to understand self and make conscious decisions about one's responses to others would be seen by many as essential outcomes of an educational process. The direct relevance of emotional intelligence to educational leadership would therefore appear to have a number of manifestations.

First and foremost is the notion of the leader as exemplar, as a model of appropriate behaviour:

> Socially intelligent leadership starts with being fully present and getting in synch. Once a leader is engaged, then the full panoply of social intelligence can come into play, from sensing how people feel and why, to interacting smoothly enough to move people into a positive state.
> Excellence in people management cannot ignore [these] subterranean affective currents: they have real human consequences, and they matter for people to perform at their best. And because emotions are so contagious, every boss at every level needs to remember he or she can make matters either worse or better. (Goleman, 2006, page 280)

The natural reticence and shyness of many senior staff in schools leads them to underestimate the importance of their behaviour both as a model and as a sanction, in other words implicitly condoning certain patterns of behaviour. There is also, possibly, a tendency to minimize or downplay the impact of the emotions on the way a school works. If a school's values talk about notions of 'respect', 'community' and so on, then there has to be appropriate behaviour. The ethical imperative has to be matched by morally consistent behaviour. The ethical imperative to 'love thy neighbour' has to be matched by the moral action of the Good Samaritan. There is therefore a moral imperative on school leaders to adopt a model of personal effectiveness, which exemplifies the values of the school and models the translation of principle into practice.

The second factor is both principled and pragmatic. Decision making, even in a close relationship, is a problematic and complex process. In a school, with an almost infinite number of social permutations, it is especially difficult. It therefore behoves leaders to work to create a culture, 'the way we do things around here', which optimizes effective collaboration and enhances interpersonal relationships. Again, this is both functional – it leads to better decisions – and embodies principle in practice. The next justification lies less in theory and more in emerging fact. Our understanding of neurological functioning points increasingly to the fact that learning is an emotionally based activity. Effective brain functioning is dependent on a positive emotional environment. Anger, stress and tension will actively block appropriate brain functioning; a positive and relaxed climate will enhance the potential to learn. This applies to adults as much as it does to children. In all of the debate surrounding the concept of the learning organization (and whether schools can ever achieve that status) the importance of the emotional climate is often overlooked. This is much more than the absence of tension; it is the creation of positive self and mutual regard.

The final point focuses on educational leaders themselves. The discussion so far has tended to focus on the social environment. However, it is important to stress that the mental landscape of the individual is at least as important as the public arena. The definition of emotional intelligence offered above stressed that it starts with personal awareness and understanding and this dimension of leadership is often neglected.

> It is not enough that educational leaders show consideration for emotions and their social and emotional dimension. Within education ... emotions are a site of control and a mode of political resistance. Emotion matters in educational leadership because leaders, teachers and learners understand and enact their roles of subordination and domination significantly through learned emotional responses ... (Zorn and Boler, 2007, page 148)

Leadership effectiveness is a product of personal effectiveness, which is in turn grounded in emotional self-awareness and emotional literacy. What makes leadership distinctive is the high level of sustained and significant engagement with others. In the course of a day this can involve the extremes of anger and despair, and joy and celebration. It is worth reflecting on the number of transactions leaders have each day, each of them rich in potential, each of them a 'moment of truth' and every one of them based in perception rather than logic and rationality – or at least in competing rationalities. The level of demand and impact will, of course, vary over time and context but this aspect of the job of the leader explains why it is both so demanding and challenging and so rich and rewarding. This in turn leads to the need for emotionally literate leaders: leaders who are fluent and confident in talking about their social and emotional engagement because they have a rich personal vocabulary and understand the rules of grammar. Highly effective leaders are skilled in the syntax of relationships.

The emotionally intelligent school

Emotionally intelligent leadership might be seen as a microcosm of the emotionally intelligent school; the leader and the school are in a fractal relationship, each a scale representation of the other. However, it is obviously nonsense to talk of the organization as having human characteristics; it is necessary to discuss culture and climate in this context. In their model of RelationaLearning Otero et al. (2001) defines learning as embracing:

> . . . the human connection; connection of self to self, of self to others, and of self to content. Indeed, personal, heartfelt connection is the soul of the RelationaLearning model. (page 9)

Otero and his associates go on to argue that the conditions for mutual involvement in learning are:

- respect
- empathy
- honesty
- caring
- inviting
- exchange
- playfulness.

This list obviously has very close parallels with the characteristics of emotional intelligence identified previously. (Playfulness here is defined as full engagement with and commitment to both personal and interdependent learning.) There is nothing particularly unique or distinctive about this list until you consider the absence of any of these elements from a relationship or any form of social activity –

relationships are then immediately compromised. It is worth stressing again that these are both effective and appropriate behaviours, with a portfolio of relevant skills, and the basis of a moral life.

A further reinforcement and extension of this approach is provided by Bryk and Schneider (2002), who argue that trust is a prerequisite to learning and academic success and they identify the components of trust as:

- respect
- competence
- personal regard
- integrity.

In their research into schools in Chicago, Bryk and Schneider found a high correlation between the levels of trust in a school and its capacity to improve. Schools with a high level of trust, at the outset of a programme to improve maths and reading, had a 1 in 2 chance of improving. Schools with relatively low levels of trust had only a 1 in 7 chance of improving. Schools in the latter category which did improve made significant gains in their levels of trust as a prerequisite to raising attainment. The authors describe trust as the 'connective tissue' that binds schools together and this image helps to reinforce the importance of healthy neural and social networks to effective learning. In essence this is all about building social capital, creating learning communities that are exemplified in the strength of social networks, interdependency, engagement, shared purpose, parity of esteem and genuine reciprocity. Covey (2006) is unambiguous about the status and role of trust in personal and organizational life:

> When trust is high, the dividend you receive is like a performance multiplier ... In a company high trust materially improves communication, collaboration, execution, innovation ... In your personal life, high trust significantly improves your excitement, energy, passion, creativity and joy in your relationships ... (page 19)

Covey goes on to describe the various types of trust, what he classifies as the five waves of trust:

1 Self trust – personal credibility and confidence.
2 Relationship trust – consistent behaviour in personal relationships.
3 Organizational trust – designing structures and procedures around trust.
4 Market trust – working through reputation and integrity.
5 Societal trust – interdependence and commitment. (pages 34–35)

Clearly each level of trust is a function of its predecessor and the building of trust is a cumulative process, and this again reinforces the importance of leaders modelling in order to enable others to adopt alternative ways of behaving. The emotionally intelligent school might be said to have the following characteristics:

1 Building emotional literacy – developing a shared vocabulary to understand self and others and enable dialogue.
2 Regular dialogue around the key emotional responses:
    – anger, fear, hate, love, jealousy, excitement, failure, success, grief.
3 Developing a shared portfolio of skills and strategies:
    – empathy, conflict management, negotiation, active listening, respect for others, respect for self, expressing emotions, problem solving, showing respect and acceptance.
4 Building explicit links between school values, culture and policies and daily routines and behaviour.
5 Investing in building trust, sophisticated networks.
6 Leaders modelling appropriate behaviours and supporting review, monitoring and evaluation followed by interventions as needed.
7 Learners actively involved in all of the above.

Transformation of education systems will not take place except in a context of high emotional literacy, notably trust – transformation is a highly emotional process; it requires emotional intelligence if the old ways are to be abandoned (bearing in mind that the old ways are personal histories and life stories) and new ways adopted (remembering that they are potentially unproven and a denial of perceived prior success). Such a change cannot be a wholly rational process – in fact it is doubtful if change is ever rational in the sense of being logical, predictable, measurable and controllable. Change can never really be managed, it is never linear, and this is even more the case with transformation.

How can we develop and sustain emotional intelligence?

Emotional intelligence cannot be taught. It is not developed through one-off events and by definition does not lend itself to distance or virtual education. In essence it is about enhancing a person's human capacity. It might be helpful to think of this capacity as a reservoir (this metaphor is developed in more detail in Chapter 6); each day it is drawn on, and on many days it is replenished. However, there will be times when the demand is so high that levels get dangerously low – with potentially dangerous consequences. Leadership development has to focus on strategies to refill the reservoir and keep it in a state of equilibrium by developing emotional literacy so that personal understanding can be communicated in meaningful ways. One of the most important of these is openness, the willingness and ability to articulate honestly and accurately to another exactly how one is feeling – especially in response to them. This is where status and roles, gender, culture, skills and norms all come into play. The ability to articulate an emotional response to a colleague is not yet, in many schools, 'taken for granted' behaviour. Equally, emotional responses in the classroom can be seen, still, as disciplinary matters rather than relational, with implications for all those involved. It is still worth questioning the extent to which the open authentic expression of anger, frustration, disappointment, anxiety or fear is treated with appropriate respect in most English classrooms. If there is to be emotional security in any learning or leadership environment then there will have to be shared protocols, a common language and high confidence based on internalized behaviours and skills which enable authentic responses rather than shallow reactions.

In this context it might be helpful to think about the mode of learning that is appropriate, as shown in Table 5.1.

Table 5.1 Modes of learning

Shallow	Deep	Profound
Information	Knowledge	Wisdom
Replication	Understanding	Meaning
Memorisation	Reflection	Intuition
Extrinsic	Intrinsic	Moral

Source: adapted from West-Burnham and Coates, 2005, page 35

Emotional intelligence requires deep and profound learning, which is concerned with the creation of personal wisdom and meaning, the development of the capacity to act intuitively and a recognition that the motivation to learn in this way has to be moral. At the heart of the movement, away from shallow and superficial espousals of the importance of interpersonal relationships to genuine engagement with emotional intelligence, is the process of understanding; converting generic information into personal knowledge that informs action.

Profound learning is therefore rooted in personal change and growth; it is about the development of personal models, or mind maps, which both inform and interpret behaviour. The learning strategies associated with this approach might include:

1 Systematic and structured reflection.

2 Coaching, mentoring and critical friendship.

3 Focused review and feedback.

4 Theory building and testing.

5 Team-based learning.

6 The creation of a community of practice.

However, these suggestions only have validity if there is a predisposition to learn. Thus we have to include in any definition of leadership effectiveness a willingness to learn and an understanding of how that learning takes place. As Fullan (2001) expresses it:

> If you want to develop leadership, you should focus on reciprocity, the mutual obligation and value of sharing knowledge among organisational members. The key to developing leadership is to develop knowledge and share it. (page 132)

The bases of leadership are reciprocity and sharing, which are also the bases of leadership development and they are also the simplest definition of emotional intelligence. To learn effectively the individual has to be emotionally intelligent; this means he or she has to live and work in an emotionally intelligent environment, which in turn means that there has to be emotionally intelligent leadership in depth.

6 Leadership and spirituality

School leadership can be one of the most rewarding, satisfying and fulfilling jobs that it is possible to think of. It has the potential for enormous satisfaction – it can be challenging, creative, stimulating and great fun. At its best, school leadership offers enormous scope for making things happen, being innovative and, most significantly perhaps, making a real and profound difference to the lives of students and colleagues. Over time, school leaders have the opportunity to see real and tangible results for their efforts. The work of educators is often frustrated by a whole range of factors outside their control but there are many occasions when they know that they have changed a life for the better.

Leadership involves all in the school community: the essential acts of effective leadership are not restricted to those in power; there cannot be a hierarchy of leadership significance:

> The distributed capacity for spiritual experience underlines the fact that the potential for wisdom and vision does not rest solely with positional leaders. Transformational leadership which genuinely aspires to raise everyone towards higher ethical aspirations ... needs to recognise the importance of dispersed empowerment which supports the participation and values the potential of all voices ... In other words, spiritual resources and understanding are dispersed ... (Woods, 2007, page 152)

Wisdom and vision are not the exclusive preserve of those in charge, and spiritual depth is not correlated with age, experience or status. However, even in the most auspicious environments, the job of school leader can be challenging and demanding. Every day requires numerous interpersonal transactions – some challenging, some profoundly rewarding and others mind-numbingly tedious and routine. Yet all are significant in some way. There are days of endless negotiations, managing inadequate resources and seeking to mediate negative external forces. And there are times when, in spite of every best effort, it seems that the job is akin to that of Sisyphus – condemned to spend each day pushing a rock to the top of the hill only to see it roll down and having to repeat the task the following day. But then there are opportunities for genuine transformation – of the individual, the institution and the system. Those times when moral purpose and professional aspiration are translated into concrete actions that make a demonstrable difference and when it is clear that transformation is taking place.

In reality, the lives of most school leaders fall between these extremes: there are the routines and the established patterns and rhythms of school life; there are the daily rewards of observing the brilliantly taught lesson, the moment of breakthrough when understanding emerges, the unexpected letter of thanks and the opportunity to change a life. What does remain constant is the disproportionate impact that the language, values and behaviour of school leaders have upon their school. We know from personal experience and research done on new headteachers and changes in the leadership of schools in challenging circumstances that leadership can have an impact which is directly attributable to the leadership style of one individual. It is both a strength and a weakness of our education system that so much influence is vested in one individual. This raises the questions of 'Who cares for the carer?'; 'Who coaches the coach?'; 'Who counsels the counsellor?'; 'How is leadership sustained?' It is the issue of sustainability that is perhaps most taxing. What is it that gives some people their resilience, their ability to 'bounce back', their often intimidating optimism and capacity to maintain a relentless pace and level of engagement?

One of the dominant characteristics of highly effective leaders is their personal authenticity – their personal and professional integrity, the sense that they are working because of personal values and conviction. The credibility of leaders is often directly related to their perceived consistency. The combination of all these factors places a significant burden on leaders – just how do they keep going and what enables them to remain creative? We know that school leadership has a real cost. However rewarding the job, it requires enormous reserves of personal, emotional, physical and intellectual stamina to keep going day after day, term after term, year after year. Like all true professionals, school leaders recognize that there is an altruistic dimension to their work. School leadership at its most effective is demanding and draining. In essence, there has to be a balance between demands and returns, between the positive and negative and, perhaps, we need to see this as at least as significant a factor as any other component of effective leadership. Authenticity is a product of depth; it is the expression of personal understanding.

For a host of cultural and historical reasons we have tended to neglect the inner-lives of leaders. It has always been seen as 'too personal' to make public but, I would argue, we continue to neglect it at our peril. The sustainability, resilience, effectiveness and well-being of leaders are directly related to the health of the 'inner-self'.

Personal authenticity, moral confidence and professional courage are direct indicators of personal wholeness.

A convenient way of capturing this dimension of personal and professional life is to talk of spirituality. Not in a specifically religious sense, nor in a vague reference to that which cannot be explained by other means, but in the sense of that which makes us fully human:

> I assimilate the notion of [the] spiritual to an intense experience of harmony, to the sense that the organism is functioning with the greatest possible perfection. The experience unfolds in association with the desire to act towards others with kindness and generosity. Thus to have a spiritual experience is to hold sustained feelings of a particular kind dominated by joy, however serene. (Damasio, 2003, page 284)

This is the idea of spirituality as an element of being human which is common to all societies and cultures but expressed in many different ways, some religious and some secular. This is to engage with the existential, ideas of perfection, engagement with others: those aspects of our sense of self that are most fundamental. To recognize the spiritual dimension in our lives is to recognize that we are more than just the products of our genes and environments, more than a range of physically conditioned responses or intellectual constructs; we are the synthesis of all of these elements – a classic example of the whole being more than the sum of the parts:

> If you can approach the world's complexities, both its glories and its horrors, with an attitude of humble curiosity, acknowledging that however deeply you have seen, you have only just scratched the surface, you will find worlds within worlds, beauties you could not heretofore imagine, and your own mundane preoccupations will shrink to proper size ... (Dennett, 2006, page 303)

It is to recognize that which makes us unique as human beings, that which gives us value and that which shapes our identity and sense of self; it helps achieve a sense of place and context and it is about a sense of joy. It is very much about who I am as a person, but it is equally concerned with my relationship with others and with the world that we inhabit and share.

> At the very minimum, spirituality is the subtle and not easily specifiable awareness that surrounds virtually everything and anything that transcends our petty self-interest ... Spirituality, I want to argue, is an expanded form of the self ... (Solomon, 2002, page 12)

Spirituality is thus about understanding who I am, who you are, who we are and how we relate to each other, those aspects of the human experience that seem to transcend all relationships and that which nurtures and sustains us through the shared experience of delight, pain and sorrow, and those elements of our lives that transcend all of these factors. I want to use the idea of the spiritual in this context to cover:

- the sense of what makes us unique and distinctive as a person;
- our ability to seek to engage with that which is eternal, enduring and true;
- our understanding of ourselves in relation to others;
- our capacity to love, care, and show compassion and empathy;
- that which sustains our moral purpose and focuses our sense of justice and courage;
- that which allows us to feel and express joy, wonder and exhilaration;
- that which gives us hope;
- our engagement with the numinous: the transcendent.

In other words, the dimension of our lives that creates meaning. For some this meaning may be found through one of the great faiths, for others in a systematic philosophy or (as is often the case) through a personal amalgamation of many disparate elements drawing on historical and cultural sources and personal relationships as avenues for the expression of self. It is impossible to assemble an ideal 'inventory' of what constitutes meaning for each person; the spiritual dimension is expressed in many different ways: in the search for eternal truths, the struggle for social justice, in scientific discovery, in artistic creativity, in professional commitment, the exploration of ideas and the love of others. The psychologist and philosopher William James argued that:

> ... a person's *spiritual self* may be regarded as a set of 'psychic dispositions', including the abilities to argue and discriminate and to have 'moral sensibility', 'conscience', and an 'indomitable will'. Alternatively, he elaborated, one's spiritual self can be seen as the entire stream of our personal consciousness. (Martin and Baressi, 2006, page 297)

In broad terms, it might be possible to identify a number of parallel pathways that help us to understand the place of the spiritual in personal growth and development and so in leadership effectiveness. Spirituality might be seen as:

- The search for the existential self, the journey towards enlightenment and the development of personal potential.
- The search for truth in the sense of engaging with the most basic and challenging questions about the nature of human existence, the mystery of creation and the nature (and existence) of a supreme being or fundamental force.

- The search for justice in recognizing and respecting the integrity and dignity of every human life and securing a shared entitlement to human rights and freedoms, for example happiness and well-being.
- The search for community, creating recognition, respect and acceptance for the numerous ways in which human beings can express their social needs and celebrate their lives together.
- The search for opportunities to serve to enhance the lives of others, to find personal understanding through a sense of vocation.
- The search for creativity expressed in many wonderfully different ways in the creative and performing arts, in technology and in social relationships – seeking new means of self-expression.

One only has to listen to people who have achieved a level of personal understanding to recognize the attributes of spiritual meaning in their lives. They have a rich and sophisticated vocabulary, they can explain and share their understanding, their language is authentic (words match actions) and, crucially, they are constantly revisiting, confirming and developing the basis of their personal meaning. And so in the lives of painters and dancers (and those who paint and dance), novelists and physicists, those involved in the care of the terminally ill, those who help the learning of the very youngest and the most disabled, there are opportunities for exploring the spiritual. It is not just about church, mosque, synagogue, temple or 'special places'.

> The work of authentic educational leaders is transformational insofar as they promote and support transformational teaching and learning for their students. To do this they must bring their deepest principles, beliefs, values and convictions to their work. The ethic of authenticity is at the very heart and soul of educational leadership ... (Duignan, 2006, page 131)

If we see leadership as a full expression of humanity, rather than a set of simplistic outcomes, skills and techniques, then we need to take the spiritual dimension as seriously as any other aspect of leadership development. If effective, high performance leadership is to be sustained over time then it needs a deep, sophisticated and rich underpinning. The trees that survive the drought are those with the deepest root systems. If the following extract from Paulo Freire is read from the specific perspective of educational leadership rather than his generic focus on educators then a very powerful model of authenticity emerges:

> Hence the exigency they must impose on themselves of growing ever more tolerant, of waxing ever more open and forthright, of turning ever more critical, of becoming ever more curious.
>
> The more tolerant, the more open and forthright, the more critical, the more curious and humble they become, the more authentically they will take up the practice of teaching. (Freire, 1992, page 67)

One image that some have found helpful in this very challenging and demanding context is the idea of the 'reservoir of hope'. This is:

> ... the calm centre at the heart of the individual leader, 'the still point in the turning world' from which their value and vision flows and which continues to allow effective interpersonal engagement and sustainability of personal and institutional self-belief in the face of draining external pressures and challenging critical incidents in the life of the school. (Flintham, 2008, page 58)

Hope is one of the most powerful human qualities; in many ways all of the various manifestations of spirituality described above are about hope. Hope is about the potential for the future, it is not just about optimism, it is about growth and resilience. Without a fundamental sense of hope we would never start on the path to transformation; education is the essential expression of hope in a society.

Think of a reservoir high in the mountains of central Wales. At one end of the long submerged valley is a dam with the technology to control the flow of the water. The rest of the lake is the most evocative and powerful combination of natural features – rock, trees and water. Around the lake people walk, sail, fish or just revel in the unspoiled beauty. All around the lake are small rivers and streams flowing down from the surrounding hills. In many ways I see this scene as a metaphor for the inner-life of transformational leaders.

Each working day school leaders have to draw on their personal reservoir – on some days a steady flow will suffice, on other days the floodgates have to be open as energy, compassion, creativity, optimism, courage and hope are called on. The deeper the reservoir, the more can be given, but eventually even the deepest reservoir will begin to run low. A period of drought can transform a rich reserve into something arid and barren, incapable of nurturing and sustaining growth. It is striking when flying over a desert landscape to see how rich and inviting the oasis is – even from 38,000 feet.

Effective leaders need strategies to ensure that their reservoirs are regularly filled – to ensure that there are lakes, streams and rivers to renew, refresh and refill. Nurturing and refilling the reservoir thus becomes crucial leadership work. It is not about being self-indulgent or selfish, it is about being selfish: having a proper and appropriate regard for personal growth and sustainability. There are as many strategies as there are people but there are some well-understood approaches that are worth exploring.

First, most obvious but most elusive, is the need for time and space. Leaders need to make appointments with themselves in their diaries. Sometimes there is the need to retreat to the warmth and security of the cave to find time to review, reflect and heal. This may involve closing the office door for 30 minutes, spending a half day at home, going to a favourite place or building – the crucial point is seeing quiet reflection as work, as part of the job. For those with a religious faith it might be that a mosque, temple, synagogue or church provides such an environment; for others it might be a favourite walk, run or swim, but in all cases it is the focus on self that is important: How am I?

A second strategy that many find helpful is engagement with a mentor, trusted colleague or, to use a concept from Celtic spirituality, the *anam cara*, the soul friend:

> In this love, you are understood as you are without mask or pretension. The superficial and functional lies and half truths of acquaintance fall away. You can be as you really are. Love allows understanding to dawn, and understanding is precious. When you are understood, you are at home. (O'Donohue, 1997, page 36)

This has echoes of Aristotle's conception of the friend as 'another self'. This relationship is about sharing, trust, openness, disclosure of hopes and fears, innermost dreams and despair. Such a relationship will find many different modes of expression from the formal professional relationship, the various guises of teacher, through friendship to the confessional and beyond. In many such relationships there are echoes of Vygotsky's models of learning as a social relationship – for many the growth of personal spiritual meaning is significantly enhanced through a social interaction; it might be that Zone of Proximal Development might be applied to spiritual growth. This is reflected, of course, in all of the world's great faiths – the spiritual guide as guru, mentor and teacher and, as George Steiner (2003) expresses it, in 'Lessons of the Masters':

> To awaken in another human being powers, dreams beyond one's own; to induce in others a love for that which one loves; to make of one's inward present their future: this is a threefold adventure like no other ... to teach, to teach well, is to be accomplice to transcendent possibility. (pages 183–184)

It may be that every leader needs a teacher, a guide or a friend. I am confident that we do not give enough status and significance to friendship – it might be that more authentic friendships will reduce the need for executive life coaches.

> ... when momentarily or over time two people form a connection unsullied by the usual ambiguous affections of life, free from the complexities of being honest, it is something that potentially stays with them for ever. (Vernon, 2005, page 159)

The third element is structured reflection – which may well be expressed in the previous two strategies. Specifically this is about making sense of experiences, celebrating and consolidating success, recognizing strengths, crucially learning from failures, and all the time integrating theory and practice, aspiration and reality, hope and experience. Many find keeping a journal a powerful tool to support this process. Reading and reflecting on appropriate texts can also help. What are important are the recognition of success and the capturing of learning – two powerful rivers to feed the reservoir. Dewey (1933) argues that reflection is directly related to moral development:

> ... open-mindedness, whole-hearted or absorbed interest, responsibility in facing consequences, are of themselves personal qualities, traits of character. They are not the only attitudes that are important in order that the *habit* of thinking in a reflective way may be developed. But the other attitudes that might be set forth are also traits of character, attitudes that, in the proper sense of the word, are *moral* ... (page 33)

Fourth, there is a range of activities which, superficially, might not seem to be closely linked to spirituality but in fact are part of the process of filling the reservoir. Sailing the boat, throwing the pot, turning the wooden bowl, singing in the choir, spending the summer working in a rural school in Botswana – all have the potential to refresh, renew and build personal resilience, a sense of joy and engagement in an activity that enhances and enriches.

Fifth, is the sense of being on a journey and taking an active and committed role in determining the nature and destination of the journey. This implies engagement in spiritual growth, and development as a deliberate and conscious act which, like any journey, is full of decisions about when, where and how to travel and, crucially, who to travel with, if anyone. The metaphor of the journey is fundamental to most of the world's great faiths and in many ways it echoes the origins of humanity – the journey out of Africa, but it also has to include the mundane journey to work each day. Being on a journey is about a willingness to change and be changed, to consider new possibilities and opportunities and to accept responsibility for the implications of the choices made. Crucially the journey is about new vistas, new ways of seeing the world and so new ways of understanding.

The penultimate strategy has to do with worship – it is about the liturgy of celebration and it can take very many forms. It is about the formality and solemnity of the religious service, it is about dancing, making music and eating together, it is in Barbara Ehrenreich's wonderful phrase about 'collective joy':

> We can live without it as most of us do, but only at the risk of succumbing to the solitary nightmare of depression. Why not reclaim our distinctively human heritage as creatures who can generate their own ecstatic pleasures out of music, color, feasting and dance? (2007, page 260)

Finally, perhaps the most important source of renewal and refreshment is quality engagement with others at work and in recreation: with the team, colleagues, students, friends, those who are loved and love in return. We are social beings and it is in the quality of our relationships that we find ourselves. It is in the shared meals, the common experiences and, crucially, in collective learning that we are most likely to become fully aware of our human potential. Even headteacher conferences are a powerful source of renewal: I often feel the most useful thing I do when speaking at heads' conferences is to fill the gaps between coffee and lunch where the real engagement takes place.

Sustainability is about hope: hope is not available on courses; it comes from our wholeness and authenticity as people. This dimension transcends jobs and roles, skills and capabilities. However expressed it is about the joy of learning and becoming fully human. Perhaps the simplest form of reflection to support the refilling of the reservoir is to ask two simple questions: 'What joy do I get from my work?' and 'What joy for others have I created through my work?' For it is often in the valuing and affirmation of others that we find affirmation of ourselves; leadership provides many challenges but it also provides wonderful opportunities to be 'surprised by joy'.

7

The leader as intellectual

If schools are about transforming the lives of individual students and education systems are about transforming societies, then it surely follows that the leadership of schools and systems has to be transformative:

> ... educators need to become provocateurs; they need to take a stand while refusing to be involved in either a cynical relativism or doctrinaire politics. In part, I mean that central to intellectual life is the pedagogical and political imperative that academics engage in rigorous social criticism while becoming a stubborn force for challenging false prophets, deconstructing social relations that promote material and symbolic violence, and speaking the 'truth' to dominant forms of power and authority. At the same time, as I mentioned earlier such intellectuals must be deeply critical of their own authority and how it structures classroom relations and cultural practices. (Giroux, 1997, page 268)

Thus the role of the intellectual is to provide a critique of policy and practice, to interrogate roles and relationships and to be rigorous in self-appraisal, avoiding:

> ... the fawning elasticity with regards to one's own side that has disfigured the history of intellectuals since time immemorial. (Judt, 2008, page 167)

Much of our language about leadership is derived from military or commercial cultures; therefore it is not often that the concept of the intellectual is linked to that of the leader (especially in the way that Giroux outlines above). In fact in some ways they could be seen as antithetical. Equally, in British culture the very concept of the intellectual is suspect:

> In Britain, the term 'intellectual' is widely derided. It is used by public commentators to invalidate a person's ideas as elitist and self important. (Rushdie, cited in Lévy, 2000, page 247)

According to Furedi (2003, page 16) intellectuals have an 'image problem' and terms such as 'nerd, geek, egghead and wonk' demonstrate that people who care about knowledge are 'not cool'. And there are stern warnings for those who might contemplate engaging with intellectuals:

> ... beware intellectuals. Not merely should they be kept well away from the levers of power, they should also be objects of particular suspicion when they seek to offer collective advice. Beware committees, conferences and leagues of intellectuals ... we must at all times remember what intellectuals habitually forget: that people matter more than concepts and must come first. The worst of all despotisms is the heartless tyranny of ideas. (Johnson, 1988, page 342)

One of the most negative stereotypes of the intellectual is the individual who is so obsessed with ideas that everything else is marginalized and diminished, except his or her own ego needs; we live:

> In an age of self-promoting media intellectuals, vacantly preening before the admiring mirror of their electronic audience. (Judt, 2008, page 104)

By and large the British do not trust intellectuals; it is something the French do:

> ... anyone who takes the trouble to be sufficiently thrusting can give himself undue prominence by an aggressive assumption of continental intellectual manners. (Collini, 2006, page 583)

Intellectuals are odd, they even look different:

> Sometimes, in our century, the definition has been expanded to include anyone wearing spectacles, or reading a magazine. Sometimes it has included anyone with fillings in his teeth. When tyranny is born, people like these often die. (Rushdie, cited in Lévy, 2000, page 247)

It is easy to parody the concept of intellectual. Equally, the absence of the concept from much of the debate about the nature of leadership is symptomatic of the marginal status of the role and nature of the intellectual. And yet if all of the implications of the preceding chapters are brought together then they point to the need for leaders who are capable of moving beyond prevailing norms and patterns, who are prepared to question orthodoxy and challenge received wisdom.

> Regardless of individual temperament, intellectuals are often forced to challenge contemporary wisdom, and convention. (Furedi, 2004, page 34)

> Being an intellectual implies social engagement. It is difficult to live for ideas and not attempt to influence society. It involves not only being involved in creative mental activity, but also the assumption of social responsibility and taking a political stand. (Furedi, 2004, page 35)

> By 'intellectual,' I mean the 'free' intellectual, someone who, beyond his or her professional or technical or artistic expertise, is committed to exercising (and thereby, implicitly, defending) the life of the mind as such. (Sontag, cited in Lévy, 2000, page 253)

The work of the intellectual in society might thus be seen in terms of questioning and challenging; engaging with social and political action and accepting personal responsibility for the debate about the nature of society, in other words the intellectual as a social activist working through a concern for ideas and concepts and, crucially, comfortable in debate and dialogue about them. For Edward Said (1994), the work of the intellectual can be summarized as:

- Love for, and an unquenchable interest in, the larger picture.
- Making connections.
- Refusing to specialize.
- Caring for ideas and values.
- Speaking the truth to power.

Uniting these elements is the belief that intellectuals are committed to a rational world view; they are the descendants of the thinkers of the eighteenth century who argued for reason and logic in the face of dogma, superstition and prejudice.

> Despite their quarrelsome diversity, however, most Enlightenment thinkers shared certain intellectual traits – an insistence on intellectual autonomy, a rejection of tradition and authority as the infallible sources of truth, a loathing for bigotry and persecution, a commitment to free inquiry, a belief that (in Francis Bacon's words) knowledge is indeed power ... The Enlightenment had many critics, but its illuminating influence and achievements were apparent in the history of the next two centuries – the waning of absolutism and superstition, the rise of secular democracy, the understanding of the natural world, the transformation of historical and scientific study, the new political resonance of notions such as 'progress', 'rights' and 'freedom'. (Wheen, 2004, pages 5–6)

It is in these latter respects that the link between the role of the intellectual and the role of the leader might begin to become clear. The intellectual traits that Wheen identifies would seem to me to be a powerful set of criteria for moral leadership in general and for leadership in educational context specifically:

The creative role of an intellectual requires detachment from any particular identity and interest. Since the beginning of modernity, the authority of the intellectual has rested on the claim to be acting and speaking on behalf of society as a whole. The intellectual can be seen as the personification of the Enlightenment legacy and has traditionally sought to represent the standpoint of universality. (Furedi, 2004, page 34)

The intellectual thus has a responsibility that transcends time and place; there is an overarching commitment to broaden human values and concerns, and to issues that go beyond the concerns of short-term issues of employment and personal status. The intellectual has a duty to set in context, to establish relationships, and to point out inconsistencies and illogicalities. Crucially the role of the intellectual is never to accept at face value and to reserve the right to question and challenge:

One is an intellectual because one has (or should have) certain standards of probity and responsibility in discourse. That is the one indispensable contribution of intellectuals: the notion of discourse that is not merely instrumental, i.e. conformist. (Sontag, cited in Lévy, 2000, page 253)

One of the issues with intellectuals in Britain is that they do not seem to have 'proper jobs'. They often appear to be members of a self-appointed, self-referential and self-perpetuating elite whose role is to pass judgement on the key issues of the day (usually in the morning on Radio 4 or late at night on BBC2) in a way that is sufficiently arcane and recondite to reassure listeners that somebody understands the issue, therefore they do not have to. However, the Italian Marxist theoretician Gramsci argues that everyone is an intellectual because they carry:

... on some form of intellectual activity, that is, he is a 'philosopher', and artist, a man of taste, he participates in a particular conception of the world, has a conscious line of moral conduct, and therefore contributes to sustain a conception of the world or to modify it, that is, to bring into being new modes of thought. (Forgacs, 1999, page 321)

Gramsci democratizes the intellectual, engaging in the world is an intellectual act; an intellectual is anyone that belongs to a group that has:

... to think and inquire for itself, if necessary outside the confines of received or imposed wisdom. Journalists, doctors, lawyers, scientists, philosophers, teachers, writers are all covered by this definition. (Rushdie, cited in Lévy, 2000, pages 246–247)

If Rushdie is correct, then many prevailing views of the role and status of teachers will have to be questioned and we will have to accept that:

> ... teachers are bearers of critical knowledge, rules, and values through which they consciously articulate and problematize their relationship to each other, to students, to subject matter, and to the wider community. Such a view of authority challenges the dominant view of teachers as technicians or public servants, whose role is primarily to implement rather than conceptualize pedagogical practice. (Giroux, 1997, page 103)

Giroux's view of teaching as a socially problematic activity, in which the various participants have to work to reconcile competing perceptions and expectations, is further complicated by Said's view that not only is the role of the teacher as technician or public servant problematic; so is the idea of the teacher as professional:

> By professionalism I mean thinking of your work as an intellectual as something you do for a living, between the hours of nine and five with one eye on the clock, and another cocked at what is considered to be proper, professional behaviour – not rocking the boat, not straying outside the accepted paradigms or limits, making yourself marketable and above all presentable, hence uncontroversial and unpolitical and 'objective.' (Said, 1996, page 74)

According to Giroux and Said, teaching is not just a matter of delivering lessons, teaching a class, assessing students' work or contributing to the management and administration of the school. It is about recognizing that teaching is an activity that explicitly and implicitly translates a range of ideological perspectives into the daily experience of students and in so doing demonstrates a particular ideological stance. If this is true of teachers, then it has profound implications:

> The concept of teacher as intellectual carries with it the imperative to judge, critique, and reject those approaches to authority that reinforce a technical and social division of labor that silences and disempowers both teachers and students. (Giroux, 1997, page 103)

The implications for school leaders are equally profound:

> School leaders who are public intellectuals are willing to engage in critical self-reflection as well as to critically interrogate institutions, such as schools, in order to uncover as well as construct strategies to combat the rituals and forms of institutionalized oppression these organizations perpetuate.

> These are the scholars 'whose function is to disrupt and intervene in conversa-
> tions in ways that are disturbing and that force people to ask why they frame the
> questions in the way that they do or why they make the analysis they do'.

And

> ... freeing students to inquire and interrogate the traditionally accepted purposes
> of schools and the curriculum that supports them. (Dantley and Tillman, 2006, page
> 21)

If we are serious about transformation then it may well be that we need to move to a situation that takes the issues raised above as the starting point for a new model of leadership.

> This means that such educators are not merely concerned with forms of empow-
> erment that promote individual achievement and traditional forms of academic
> success. Instead, they are also concerned in their teaching with linking empower-
> ment – the ability to think and act critically – to the concept of social transforma-
> tion. (Giroux, 1997, page 103)

It is difficult to see how the transition from improvement to transformation can be made without the critical rigour and systematic approaches advocated by the various writers above. However, it is not enough just to advance the idea of the leader as intellectual; a more detailed and systematic model is required. A survey of the various sources cited above provides a range of possible qualities and behaviours that might be associated (but not exclusively) with an intellectual disposition. It then becomes possible to advance a model or conceptual framework of what might be described the qualities of intellectual leadership which might include: intellectual courage, intellectual curiosity, confidence in reason and intellectual humility.

Intellectual courage

This involves, first, the willingness to question received wisdom and academic authority. For example, many assumptions about the organization of schooling are based on false and damaging ideas about intelligence. Such ideas include the notion that intelligence is fixed and largely inherited, that it can be measured accurately and definitively, and that it is possible to predict future academic performance on such measurements. A modern consensus would argue that all of these are false assumptions based on bad science of the early twentieth century and that they should not be used as the basis of professional practice in education.

There are numerous examples of educational practices that are based on erroneous, superseded or bad research and practice. Think of the complex history of the provision for children with special needs and how both theory and practice have changed but still have a long way to go in terms of parity of esteem and equity. The same issue applies to the provision for the early years. Why is it that early year's provision is relatively under-resourced, but more significantly is of lower professional status – so that a graduate in philosophy with first class honours can be told that working in primary education would be a waste of his or her talents? It is for the intellectual to raise and question the uncritical acceptance of these artificial and damaging hierarchies and others like them.

Intellectual leadership also involves leaders being able to review, question and analyse their own beliefs and the implications for themselves and others of the stances they take and the positions they hold. And, if appropriate, to publicly acknowledge errors and mistakes and correct them. This links directly to the previous discussions about moral leadership and personal authenticity. Intellectual courage in educational leadership is about creating a culture in which the search for equity and excellence takes priority over the position in the league table. However, it is also, tragically, about physical courage. It is about the primary school headteacher in Afghanistan beheaded in his school's playground for refusing to stop teaching girls. It is about those teachers and school leaders who always seem to be among the first victims of ethnic cleansing and genocide.

> Totalitarian societies first burn the books; then they humiliate the scholars; then they kill those who do not buckle under. As the events of the past century remind us, a Dark Age can always descend upon us. (Gardner, 2006, page 234)

It is about the courage, over 30 years, of teachers and school leaders in Northern Ireland who made their schools safe places and who sometimes went against faith, politics and community to preserve their professional integrity and defend the rights and preserve the safety of children and young people.

Intellectual curiosity

Intellectual curiosity is about the open-minded search for truth, the desire to understand and make sense of an increasingly complex world and to share in the creation of knowledge. This is about the willingness to cross professional boundaries, to learn from and with other disciplines, to engage with other cultures and to relate these back to personal beliefs and practice. Intellectual curiosity is fundamental to creativity and innovation and therefore a precursor to transformation. The effective leader combines the ability to combine and distil knowledge with the ability to apply in new ways in a new context:

> The synthesizer seeks order, equilibrium, closure; the creator is motivated by uncertainty, surprise, continual challenge and disequilibrium. We may appropriate a famous distinction put forth by Friedrich Nietzsche. The synthesizer is Apollonian; possessed of a restrained temperament, she proceeds in a harmonious, balanced fashion. In contrast the creator is Dionysian; of a tempestuous nature, she is poised to wrestle with the gods. (Gardner, 2006, pages 98–99)

Gardner goes on to argue that for leaders the '360-degree searchlight mind' (page 100) is more appropriate and valued that the sharply focused mind and that only the rare leader, 'the transformative or visionary leader – displays genuine creativity' (page 100). All of this implies leaders who are able and comfortable in working beyond their personal academic/subject inheritance – in other words, moving beyond their intellectual 'comfort zone' and world view.

The intellectually curious leader will read Jared Diamond's study 'Collapse' rather than the latest tome on school improvement. It has more to say about the nature of community cohesion, social renewal and regeneration than almost all the technical texts on the subject. The curious leader will go and work as an adviser to school leaders in the developing world rather than spend time reinforcing what is known about schools in the developed world. The intellectually motivated leader will spend time working in an early years environment, in a Pupil Referral Unit or with students with profound learning difficulties, or will work with young men in custody, with the sixth formers of the most prestigious school available, with young soldiers just back from Afghanistan – anything to understand the learning process from a different perspective. This leader will shadow politicians, serve as a governor or a trustee of a charity, spend two weeks a year doing anything that is nothing to do with leading a school – how about a conservation project in the Maldives? (Except if he or she is learning, growing and being refreshed then it is everything to do with leading a school.) Perhaps this leader might even consider writing a book – an interesting and diverting intellectual challenge.

Confidence in reason

The leader as intellectual is committed to analysis, explanation and justification and works through logic and evidence rather than dogma and opinion. Almost by definition, intellectually rooted leadership is a rational process in which the leader works through, and models a reason-based approach. Thus in Gramsci's terms:

> The mode of being of the new intellectual can no longer consist in eloquence, which is an exterior and momentary mover of feelings and passions, but in active participation in practical life, as constructor, organizer, 'permanent persuader' and not just a simple orator … from technique-as-work one proceeds to technique-as-

science and to the historical humanistic conception without which one remains a 'specialist' and does not become a 'leader'. (Forgacs, 1999, pages 321–322)

'Technique-as-science' implies a rigorous, systematic and objective approach to decision making mediated by the 'humanistic conception'. Thus it is an approach which balances evidence and data with values and an awareness of the human implications of decision making.

> Individuals who think scientifically are aware how difficult it is to ferret out causes; they do not confuse correlation (A occurs before B) with causation (A caused B); and they are aware that any scientific consensus is subject to being overthrown. (Gardner, 2006, pages 27–28)

In arguing for a 'disciplined mind', Gardner argues that there are four essential steps:

1 Identify the fundamental concepts of the discipline in terms of content, in other words subject knowledge, and methodological, in other words systems and techniques.
2 Study the above in depth from a range of perspectives.
3 Use multiple learning and teaching strategies in order to secure genuine understanding.
4 Set up 'performances of understanding' so that learners can demonstrate their 'mastery'. (pages 32–35)

Planning becomes a process in which the potential tyranny of the rationalistic imperative and a totally unjustifiable confidence in the linearity, predictability and controllability of the process is replaced by a balance of logic and intuition. Persuasion, influencing and negotiating replace the imperative of bureaucratic structures and relationships. Historically and culturally the leader has often been represented as prophet, the arbiter of truth and definitive authority about where to go and how to get there – this has long been challenged:

> . . . what emerges most unmistakably about Socrates is his relentless questioning. If the prophetic culture is founded on the authority of 'I-say-unto-you,' this culture is based on probing precisely that foundation. It replies to the prophet, 'Why should I accept your "I-say-unto-you"? On what basis do you know what you say you know?' . . . The dynamic at work is centred in the process of questioning. (O'Malley, 2004, page 77)

The intellectual leader is more Socrates than Moses, even though people would often prefer a Mosaic figure to lead them out of the wilderness, rather than ask them how they think they got there in the first place.

Intellectual humility

The true intellectual leader never allows his or her commitment to transformation to cloud the fact that there may be alternative perspectives and that, to paraphrase the Rule of St Benedict, 'On vital matters the Abbot always consults with the Novices'. Transformation is such a complex and elusive process that is has to be remembered that there are always multiple perspectives at work and the wise leader seeks out, acknowledges and respects and then responds to alternative ways of interpreting reality. There is no such thing as absolute objectivity, only less subjectivity. The true leader as intellectual has a profound respect for the insights, knowledge and perspectives of others, be they 5 or 50.

> Teachers need to define themselves as transformative intellectuals who act as radical teachers and educators. Radical teacher as a category defines the pedagogical and political role teachers have within the schools while the notion of radical education speaks to a wider sphere of intervention in which the same concern with authority, knowledge, power, and democracy redefines and broadens the political nature of their pedagogical task, which is to teach, learn, listen, and mobilize in the interest of a more just and equitable social order. By linking schooling to wider social movements, teachers can begin to redefine the nature and importance of pedagogical struggle and in doing so provide the basis to fight for forms of emancipator authority as a foundation for the establishment of freedom and justice. (Giroux, 1997, pages 112–113)

8 Leading learning communities

The history of school improvement is essentially the history of the autonomous school led by the autonomous (and personally accountable) school leader. Most systematic approaches to school improvement focused on improving the performance of the individual school by providing it with support to meet the generic criteria for effective schools. The extremes of this approach – most notably in England – resulted in the use of league tables as an incentive to improve, in other words improvement driven by competition. While there are individual schools that have been able to respond to this pressure in a positive way across the system as a whole, it does seem to have come to an impasse. Even with a limited, reductionist and inappropriate measure of improvement (or because of it) some schools seem unable to progress. There comes a point when 'we have tried everything and nothing works'. There may be a limit as to how much any human enterprise can be improved; improvement, by definition, works on an established system or model and seeks to develop it, it does not question the fundamental assumptions underpinning the design of the system. For example, if your purpose is to make aeroplanes go faster then there is much that can be done to improve the propeller. In terms of the underlying mathematics and physics, the materials used and the design of the aircraft, significant improvements can be made. However, the laws of nature determine the limits to the speed of propeller driven aircraft. The answer is the jet engine – which is conceptually quite distinct to the propeller.

For education there might be the point at which there is a need to move from improvement to transformation. As was argued in Chapter 1, this will require rethinking of a number of long-held assumptions about the process of improvement. Of these changes perhaps the most significant is the move from the strivings of the individual to collaborative strategies. But it would be wrong to underestimate the challenges involved in moving from an individualistic to collaborative culture:

> Due to the changes in the school system and the resulting market orientation (the number of pupils has a direct impact on the size of the budget allocated to the school), there has been intense competition among schools for the last two decades. (Pont et al., 2008, page 15)

> Many educationalists claim that these ranking lists have had an unfortunate influence on public perceptions. Certainly, the consequences for the individual school, as well as for the individual pupil, are often negative, and it is clear that the construction of the tables favours schools that are already advantaged. (page 15)

The principles and practice of structural collaboration are discussed in detail in Collarbone and West-Burnham (2008). This chapter focuses on the collaborative strategies necessary to achieve transformation. Although there are many examples of schools working together and the personal 'professional generosity' of individual teachers, the very nature of schools almost compels isolation. Many teachers spend their days working in isolation from other adults; middle leaders have to focus on their own areas of responsibility and school leaders are driven to focus on 'the operational' rather than the strategic. The combination of these factors reinforces and exacerbates the historical need (in the Anglo-Saxon world) to create distinctive school cultures and identities. This in turn leads to:

- school improvement strategies focused on the individual institution;
- accountability focused on individual performance;
- the demands and challenges of running individual schools.

One way of understanding the implications of this situation is to apply Putnam and Feldstein's (2003) concept of bonding – the means by which communities (however defined) establish their integrity, identity and sense of community:

> Some networks link people who are similar in crucial respects and tend to be inward-looking – bonding social capital. Others encompass different types of people and tend to be outward-looking – bridging social capital ... Bonding social capital is a kind of sociological Super Glue, whereas bridging social capital provides a sociological WD-40. (page 2)

> The problem is that bridging social capital is harder to create than bonding social capital – after all, birds of a feather flock together. (page 3)

It may be that education systems are more comfortable with Super Glue than with WD-40. Leadbeater (2008) demonstrates the potential implications of education systems which focus on bonding rather than bridging:

> Schools, or something like them, will remain central to education and there will be a continued push to deliver higher standards, more consistently, for all pupils, with better teaching, in better classrooms. Yet schools are out of kilter with the world children are growing up in. In a world in which everything seems to be 24/7 and on demand, schools operate with rigid years, grades, terms and timetables ... Schools are factories for learning in an economy in which innovation will be critical ... Nor are schools necessarily the most important places where children learn. Families are as important to education as school. An integrated education policy would focus on how schools interact with families, including learning supports at home, working on raising family aspirations for learning. (page 147)

So it could be argued that fundamental to any transformation strategy is openness, a willingness to share, engage with others and to learn collaboratively. The alternative is potentially too appalling to contemplate, as Diamond (2005) indicates in the conclusion to his study of the reasons for the collapse of the civilization on Easter Island:

> The parallels between Easter Island and the whole modern world are chillingly obvious ... When the Easter Islanders got into difficulties, there was nowhere to which they could flee, nor to which they could turn for help; nor shall we modern Earthlings have recourse elsewhere if our troubles increase. Those are the reasons why people see the collapse of Easter Island society as a metaphor, a worst-case scenario, for what may lie ahead of us in our own future. (page 119)

This sounds rather melodramatic, but for many communities in the developed world there is the very real danger of complete social collapse with no obvious source of help. Easter Island's social and economic infrastructure collapsed because there was nobody able or willing to question or challenge the historical imperatives of the competition to build bigger statues. The last tree on Easter Island was chopped down because of the imperatives of competition rather than collaboration.

If transformation is to be achieved then a starting point may need to be the way that educationalists view integration, collaboration and cooperation and, perhaps most importantly, shared approaches to learning and development. The potential of the process is described by Leadbeater (2008):

> An idea is set in motion by being shared. The range of tools available for pooling, exchanging and developing ideas determines the extent of our possible innovation and creativity and so fundamentally our prosperity, well-being and hope for the future. Ideas grow by being articulated, tested, refined, borrowed, amended, adapted and extended, activities that can rarely take place entirely in the head of a single individual; invariably they involve many people sharing different insights and criticisms. (page 222)

The implications of this approach are very clear:

> Cherished institutions and familiar ways of working will be threatened along with the privileged role of professional, authoritative sources of knowledge. (page 222)

An interesting example of this approach to learning and decision making relates to the overwhelming success of the Allied forces in the Second World War. In theory at least, the fascist dictatorships should have had an advantage – they could rely on:

> ... a single leader and an integrated hierarchy, making it easier to develop national unity and enthusiasm, to overcome surprise, and to act vigorously and with dispatch. (Sunstein, 2006, page 202)

In fact, as history demonstrates, this has never been the case in the long run:

> With a dictatorial regime plans are hatched in secret by a small group of partially informed men and then enforced through dictatorial authority ... By contrast, a democracy allows wide criticism and debate by many minds. (Ibid., page 202)

It is now well demonstrated that the loss of the space shuttles 'Challenger' and 'Columbia' was due to the organizational culture of NASA. What is also clear is that after the loss of 'Challenger' the culture did not change – the organization did not learn. At NASA people were pressured to follow a 'party line' and it is 'difficult for minority and dissenting opinions to percolate up through the agency's hierarchy' (Sunstein, 2006, page 13). Organizations find it difficult to learn and they conspire to prevent the people working in them from learning together.

However compelling the power, for good or ill, of organizational culture, in fact there needs to be an integrated approach to enable effective collaborative learning. Hargreaves (2003) is very clear about the components of effective learning strategies:

- identifying the main areas for transformation and securing collective ownership for them;
- creating a climate of trust among the stakeholders;
- laying down an appropriate infrastructure, both social (networks) and physical (ICT);
- encouraging schools to use this social capital to mobilise their intellectual capital in innovation;
- enhancing the organisational capital of all school leaders;
- respecting the self-organising systems and spontaneous order within the education service;
- brokering key partnerships to ensure that the process of continuous innovation and knowledge transfer thrives as the hubs change in the light of new themes and priorities for innovation. (page 73)

Hargreaves goes on to provide a powerful summary of the core task:

> Transformation requires everyone to learn: constantly, openly and quickly. (page 73)

There are many barriers and obstacles to securing the sort of open and inter-dependent learning and collaboration that Hargreaves advocates. The strength of the opposition to this integrated approach is implicitly recognized in the fifth of the principles of *The Children's Plan* (DCSF, 2007):

> services need to be shaped by and responsive to children, young people and families, not designed around professional boundaries. (pages 5–6)

The power and importance of professional boundaries should not be under-estimated. For many people they are the basis of their professional identity; indeed the basis of professional status might well be said to be the creation of boundaries or (more disparagingly) silos. This is an example of extreme bonding, where the sense of collective identity becomes more important than the clients the profession was instigated to serve. In no particular order of priority, the types of challenges that might need to be addressed in order to be confident of collaborative learning taking place include:

- The territorial imperative: school leaders as alpha-animals making and guarding their pack's territory.
- Self-legitimating bureaucratic systems: 'we do things this way because this is the way we do things'.
- Self-referential culture: the organization feeds off its own history and sense of identity to the exclusion of alternative possibilities.
- Closed language: only initiates can fully understand the language used. Acronyms and specialist usage ensure that access to knowledge is highly controlled.
- Parallel accountability: this means that each service (or silo) has its own definition of purpose, priorities and the basis on which it might be held to account.
- Competing professional identities: this is where the part or component perceives itself to be more important than the service it contributes to.
- Transactional management: managers spend their time competing for resources, working through bargaining and bolstering their personal status and power.

If a school, community or even an education system is going to commit itself to transformation, then it has to create the most auspicious circumstances possible. This implies a range of strategies that centre around the concept of learning networks and, curiously, it is old fashioned British milk bottles with aluminium tops that help to provide the answer. De Geus (1997) describes the criteria for the accelerated evolution of a species:

> By the early 1950s, the entire blue tit population of the UK – about a million birds – had learned how to pierce the aluminium seals. Regaining access to this rich food source provided an important victory for the blue tit family as a whole; it gave them an advantage in the battle for survival. Conversely the robins, as a family, never regained access to the cream.
>
> In short, the blue tits went through an extraordinarily successful institutional learning process. The robins failed, even though individual robins had been as innovative as individual blue tits ... The explanation ... could be found only in the *social propagation* process: the way blue tits spread their skill from one individual to members of the species as a whole.
>
> Birds that flock ... seem to learn faster. They increase their chances of surviving and evolving more quickly. (pages 161–162)

Innovation is fundamental to transformation but it will only have impact if the innovation is shared across a community and then applied in many different contexts. For De Geus this implies that there are high levels of job mobility with people constantly learning in different contexts, and that they work in highly inter-dependent teams with very low territorial needs but very high capacity for net-working (in other words, bridging rather than bonding). The defining characteristics of successful learning communities are:

- Innovation: Either as individuals or as a community, the species has the capacity (or at least the potential) to invent new behaviour.
- Social propagation: There is an established process for the transmission of a skill from the individual to the community as a whole ...
- Mobility: The individuals of the species have the ability to move around and (more importantly) they actually use it. (page 160)

Another way of understanding how this might work in organizations is Gloor's (2006) model of a COIN or collaborative innovation network. Gloor identifies the key elements of a COIN:

1 Collaboration networks are learning networks.
2 Collaboration networks need an ethical code.
3 Collaboration networks are based on trust and self-organization.
4 Collaboration networks make knowledge accessible to everybody.
5 Collaboration networks operate in internal honesty and transparency. (page 53)

In practice these broad principles mean that COINS:

> ... are self-organizing, unified by a shared vision, shared goals, and a shared value system. COIN members communicate with each other in a 'small world' networking structure where each team member can be reached quickly.
>
> COIN members are brought together by mutual respect and a strong set of shared beliefs. These common values act as a substitute for conventional management hierarchies, directing what every COIN member 'has to do.' COINs have internal rules by which they operate, for how members treat each other, for how supportive behavior is rewarded, and for how members are punished when they do not adhere to the code. There is a delicate internal balance of reciprocity, and a normally unwritten code of ethics with which members of the COIN comply. (Ibid., page 71)

This description of a collaborative innovation network has very powerful echoes of the guild system that dominated much of innovation, creativity and quality to manufacturing across Europe for centuries:

> The guild network provided contacts for workers on the move. Equally important, the guilds emphasized the migrant's obligations to newly encountered goldsmiths. Elaborate ritual did the work of binding the guild members to one another ... In an age when written contracts between adults had little force, when informal trust instead underpinned economic transactions, 'the single most pressing earthly obligation of every medieval artisan was the establishment of a good reputation.'
>
> For the craftsman, authority resides equally in the quality of his skills. And in the goldsmith's case, the good skills that established the master goldsmith's authority were inseparable from his ethics. (Sennett, 2008, pages 60–61)

The guilds worked through bonding and bridging, they set standards but crucially ensured the dissemination of learning by defining the necessary skills and knowledge. The culture of the guilds was essentially conservative – and this probably explains their eventual demise. In craft terms they were highly effective learning communities – in social terms they were far less effective, adopting many of the characteristics of the closed and limited communities identified above.

A more appropriate model might be found in Uglow's (2002) *The Lunar Men* – an informal but hugely influential network of the leading scientific and industrial thinkers of the late eighteenth century. The network included James Watt, Josiah Wedgwood, Matthew Bolton, Erasmus Darwin, Joseph Priestley and Samuel Galton.

> Ten of these men became Fellows of the Royal Society but only a few had a university education and most were Nonconformists or freethinkers. This placed them outside the Establishment – an apparent disadvantage which proved a real strength, since they were unhampered by old traditions of deference and stuffy

institutions. They came from varied backgrounds but when they edged towards rows they agreed to differ, turning back to the things they shared. 'We had nothing to do with the *religious* or *political* principles of each other,' wrote Priestley. 'We were united by a common love of *science* . . . Like a living unit, the group stretched to encompass the awkward and odd . . . Their passionate common exchange and endeavour was of a type that would never be possible again – until today, with the fast collaborative intimacy of the Internet. (pages xiv–xv)

The Lunar Men met monthly so that they could travel home by the light of the full moon. Their friendships lasted through generations and, crucially, they supported each other as they transformed their respective sciences and industries. Some of the defining characteristics of the Lunar Men were their openness, generosity and trust. This would seem to be a powerful formulation for any learning community as it seems to build up a critical mass which enhances learning and creativity.

A possible contemporary version of the Lunar Men is to be found in the exponents of wikinomics:

Whether designing an airplane, assembling a motorcycle, or analyzing the human genome, the ability to integrate the talents of dispersed individuals and organizations is becoming *the* defining competency for managers and firms. And in the years to come, this new mode of peer production will displace traditional corporation hierarchies as the key engine of wealth creation in the economy. (Tapscott and Williams, 2007, page 18)

The design principles underpinning the application of wikinomics provide an interesting model of a learning community:

Taking cues from your lead users
Building critical mass
Supplying an infrastructure for collaboration
Take your time to get the structures and governance right
Make sure all participants can harvest some value
Abide by community norms
Let the process evolve
Hone your collaborative mind. (Ibid., pages 286–289)

Very similar principles emerge from Putnam and Feldstein's (2003) study of successful strategies to build social capital:

- Careful analysis of the 'structural conditions', those factors which are available to support an initiative. For example, the availability of resources.
- The use of federation, 'nesting' smaller groups within larger groups to enhance a sense of belonging, commitment and to foster personal relationships.

- Fostering social ties and interdependence by developing an overarching and shared sense of belonging through common purpose and shared values.
- Building the capacity for dialogue through valuing personal and collective narratives.
- Building multi stranded networks of shared interest ...
- ... reweaving will also depend on our ability to create new spaces for recognition, reconnection, conversation and debate. (page 294)

This chapter has presented a wide range of diffuse sources that have drawn upon a range of disciplines which seem to enable some broadly compatible conclusions about the nature of effective learning communities:

- They work through consent around explicit values and clarity of purpose.
- The working culture is one of transparency, openness and sharing.
- There is a willingness to question and challenge; there is no deference to status – the culture is often iconoclastic.
- They work through highly sophisticated communication using modern technologies and traditional social and relational skills.
- There is a high degree of mutual trust, regard and friendship with a real sense of interdependence – the focus is on bonding and bridging.
- They are self-managing and self-organizing and develop strategies and protocols to support their working processes.
- They regard learning as an iterative process in which learning how to learn is as important as the focus of learning itself.
- They develop a common language with clear rules of grammar and a shared vocabulary.

A powerful example of the sort of process I am envisaging is described by David Haig in his contribution to Grafen and Ridley (2006). He is discussing Richard Dawkins' view of the nature of memes – the cultural equivalent of genes:

> The current essay is a work of propaganda. I wish to communicate ideas that I hope will influence your own concepts of genes and memes. If I am effective, you may pass on these ideas in modified form to others. In pursuit of these ends, I have crafted phrases *to grab your attention*, and have worked and reworked on clarifying concepts in my own mind ... What fraction of these ideas are my own and what fraction have been borrowed from others? The web of intellectual influence is complex and it is unclear whether I ever have a truly original idea. (page 64)

I think this is a wonderful passage which really captures the essence of collaborative learning; it is all about the web of influence in every sense of the concept of a web –

social, virtual and natural. Wenger (1998) extends and develops the idea of colla-borative learning to life in school:

> Students go to school and, as they come together to deal in their own fashion with the agenda of the imposing institution and the unsettling mysteries of youth, communities of practice sprout everywhere – in the classroom as well as on the playground, officially or in the cracks. And in spite of the curriculum, discipline and exhortation, the learning that is most personally transformative turns out to be the learning that involves membership in these communities of practice. (page 6)

I would argue that the learning that is most organizationally and socially trans-formational takes place in similar communities of practice such as the lunar society, and a scientific research community, orchestra or group of teachers working on curriculum innovation. They have most of the criteria listed above in common, most notably shared purpose and processes and a common language. What is very clear is that they are engaged in action.

Examples of possible collaborative learning strategies include:

- Small groups of headteachers on a two year development programme form action learning sets which work on real issues in real time and act as a clearing house for exploring, implementing, reviewing and developing school-focused strategies.
- ICT coordinators are given time to meet on a regular basis and compare and share strategies to support the implementation of whole-school approaches to the integration of ICT into school learning protocols.
- Extended services officers form a learning community to help them come to terms with working in a highly innovative area with no precedents or models to follow.
- School business managers develop an online resource base to share and exchange ideas about the provision of effective learning materials.
- Students from several schools come together to plan and manage a joint expedition.
- An aspiring leader programme requires participants to plan and lead a whole-school innovation project supported by mentoring by the headteacher but working in real time with real accountability.

For Wenger (1998):

> An organization's ability to deepen and renew its learning thus depends on fos-tering – or at the very least not impeding – the formation, development, and transformation of communities of practice, old and new. (page 253)

9 Leadership development and personal effectiveness

The central theme of this chapter is the vital relationship between personal effectiveness and leadership development. It is not enough to be technically competent to be an effective leader. Leadership is more than a portfolio of skills and strategies to be deployed as necessary. Effective leadership seems to be more about the person than the role. This view is reinforced by Senge et al. (2004):

> ... if you want to be a leader, you have to be a real human being. You must recognize the true meaning of life before you can become a great leader. You must understand yourself first. (page 186)

> In this sense, the cultivated self is a leader's greatest tool ... It's the journey of a lifetime. (page 186)

> That's why I think that cultivation, 'becoming a real human being', really is the primary leadership issue of our time, but on a scale never required before. (page 192)

Effective leadership is not just a job; it is a complex interaction between a range of personal and professional qualities within a context of moral purpose. Leadership can only be truly understood as moral agency; leaders are the embodiment of the principles that inform the nature of the organizations they lead. As such it is impossible to separate the personal and the professional, each informs the other. Leadership development therefore has to start with personal effectiveness.

This chapter argues for a model of leadership development that is based on the following propositions:

- Leadership development is symbiotic with personal growth.
- Effective leadership is rooted in personal authenticity.
- Authenticity is the interaction of values, language and the capacity to act.
- Becoming authentic is an emergent process – complex interactions over time.

- Complex interactions involve deep and profound learning.

Leadership is increasingly defined in terms of abstract and complex qualities. The growing focus on learning-centred leadership, the interpersonal, moral and spiritual, and future orientations of leadership has led to increased complexity and elusiveness in defining the characteristics of leaders. To some extent this is a product of the increasing emphasis being placed on the difference between leadership and management. Management is increasingly being defined in terms of concrete and operational activities that are relatively easy to learn. We need to increase our ability to develop a more meaningful and effective vocabulary to facilitate dialogue around the process of leadership learning and development. One possible way of approaching these issues is to develop a new conceptual framework to try to explain how people 'grow' into effective and successful leadership.

Such growth might be seen to have two dimensions – first, the *process* of becoming a leader and, second, recognition of leadership as a way of being, rather than a set of behaviours or outcomes. As Bennis and Goldsmith (1997) express it:

> ... the process of becoming a leader is much the same as the process of becoming an integrated human being ... leadership is a metaphor for centeredness, congruity and balance in one's life. (page 8)

Thus it might be argued that leadership development is a process of 'Self-Invention' (Bennis, 1989, page 50) which is directly linked to the creation of personal authenticity. For Taylor (1991) authenticity is about developing a personal integrity:

> Being true to myself means being true to my own originality, and that is something only I can articulate and discover. In articulating it, I am also defining myself. (page 29)

In essence, to become a leader is to become an authentic person and that involves realizing your full capacity as self. Guignon (2004) describes this as:

> ... centering in on your own inner self, getting in touch with your feelings, desires and beliefs, and expressing those feelings, desires and beliefs in all you do ... defining and realizing your own identity as a person. (page 162)

There are many ways of defining this concept of 'being a person' but the following elements would appear to be generic to most definitions:

- Understanding self in relation to others, living and working through social relationships.
- Growing through the multiple manifestations of loving and being loved, through family life and friendships (social, sexual and spiritual).
- A sense of having the capacity to achieve self-actualization and personal potential.
- The courage to behave with integrity and consistency, thus inspiring trust.
- The ability to be creative, challenge orthodoxy and innovate.
- The engagement with beauty in art and nature, from mindscapes to landscapes.

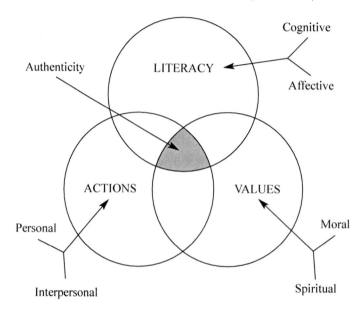

Figure 9.1 Understanding personal authenticity
Source: West-Burnham, 2007

Figure 9.1 offers a model of personal effectiveness which demonstrates the connectedness and interdependence of three elements:

1 Values: the translation of the moral and spiritual dimensions into a coherent and meaningful set of personal constructs which inform language and action. This is the personal 'mindscape' or map of the world which is how we make sense of the world we inhabit. The richer and more detailed the map the more likely we are to understand the world and our place in it.

2 Literacy: the development of a personal language which is rooted in a rich vocabulary that allows for the full expression of both the affective – the emotions and the cognitive – the intellectual.

Effective people (and leaders) are equally comfortable in engaging with the emotional and intellectual, and have the skills to communicate to achieve understanding and influence. Central to this is the notion of dialogue, the ability to hold meaningful conversations with self and others.

3 Action: the ability to use language based on values to inform personal choices and engagement with others. Equally the intrapersonal informs and enhances language and ensures that values are informing personal and social action so that there is consistency and integrity in all actions and choices.

Leadership development therefore needs to be seen as the process of becoming personally authentic. In other words, the three circles in Figure 9.1 need to overlap – the greater the level of congruity between the three elements the greater is the possibility of authenticity. The absence of any of the three elements to any significant degree will automatically compromise the possibility of authenticity.

Personal authenticity means that priority has to be given to personal effectiveness as much as professional capability. Yet for many leaders it is often the personal that is compromised. Authenticity is about personal well-being which involves the social, physical, emotional and spiritual (however defined). Becoming authentic is not an event or a destination, it is a set of complex relationships and interactions – leadership learning might be seen as recursive or iterative; it grows and changes according to context, each new development or experience has a cumulative effect and every potential source of personal growth is relevant.

The process of becoming authentic might be described as emergent, which Johnson (2001) defines as: 'The movement from low-level roles to higher level sophistication . . . ' (page 18), through a process in which the leader shows:

> . . . the distinctive quality of growing smarter over time and of responding to the specific and changing needs of [the] environment. (page 20)

Developing personal authenticity is axiomatic to developing leadership authenticity and so becoming personally and professionally effective. This involves leaders becoming deliberate and systematic in managing their learning:

> . . . we learn best when we are committed to taking charge of our own learning. Taking charge of our own learning is part of taking charge of our lives, which is the *sine qua non* of becoming an integrated person. (Bennis and Goldsmith, 1997, page 9)

The importance of this approach is reinforced by Daniel Goleman (2002):

> The crux of leadership development that works is *self-directed learning*: intentionally developing or strengthening an aspect of who you are or who you want to be, or both. This requires first getting a strong image of your *ideal self*, as well as an

accurate picture of your *real self* – who you are now. Such self-directed learning is most effective and sustainable when you understand the process of change – and the steps to achieve it as you go through it. (page 109)

There is, of course, an issue in defining what sort of learning is going to help leaders develop this model of personal authenticity. It might be helpful to draw a distinction between shallow, deep and profound learning.

In many important respects, shallow learning is synonymous with the prevailing patterns of schooling – it is based on the memorization and replication of information. Shallow learning may have been an acceptable foundation for life in a relatively simple world with fewer choices and greater hegemony, but it is clearly inadequate in a world of complex choices and limited consensus. Perhaps the most negative aspect of shallow learning is the emphasis that it places on extrinsic motivation, compliance and dependence. The learner is either a victim or lacks any sense of personal engagement – learning to lead is, in the very worst sense, an academic exercise.

Deep learning, by contrast, creates understanding – what happens when generic information becomes personal knowledge which can then be transferred between contexts and over time. Experience is understood through reflection and the motivation to learn is intrinsic. Deep learning allows personal interpretation and creates a sense of confidence through interdependent learning – notable mentoring and coaching.

Profound learning works on a different level of significance altogether. Shallow learning results in the ability to apply a formulated response to a problem, if it is presented in the right way. Deep learning allows a range of responses to be formulated, tested and applied. Profound learning leads to the problem and solution being redefined. Profound learning is about the creation of personal meaning and so enhances wisdom and hence creativity. Experience is processed intuitively. The motivation to learn is moral and the outcome of profound learning is the ability and willingness to challenge orthodoxy. Such learning is sustained through independent engagement in problem solving and thinking, which gives individuals the courage to question and to challenge. Many of the factors that contribute to profound learning are captured in Csikszentmihalyi's (1997) model of flow:

> But because almost any activity can produce flow provided the relevant elements are present, it is possible to improve the quality of life by making sure that clear goals, immediate feedback, skills balanced to action opportunities, and the remaining conditions of flow are as much as possible a constant part of everyday life. (page 34)

Profound learning is also distilled in Sternberg's (2005) definition of wisdom:

... an individual is wise to the extent he or she uses successful intelligence and experience as moderated by values to (a) seek to teach a common good for all stakeholders, (b) by balancing intrapersonal (one's own), interpersonal (others), and extrapersonal (organizational/institutional/spiritual) interests, (c) over the short and long term, to (d) adapt to, shape, and select environments. (page 358)

To move from diagnosis of self as person and leader to developing strategies for development to action which focuses on deep and profound learning requires the formulation of specific strategies. Such strategies need to meet a range of criteria:

- Build the confidence to support actions.
- Be specific to the individual.
- Enhance understanding.
- Be intrinsically motivated.
- Contribute to the development of personal wisdom.

Leadership development has to focus on the capacity to act – to translate principle into practice. In the final analysis, leadership is about relationships and the modelling of appropriate behaviours at personal and professional levels. Leadership development might thus be seen as a relationship between the need to foster authenticity and to recognize the complexity of dealing with the higher order dimensions of personal and leadership development.

Learning is a social relationship – the movement from shallow to deep learning is the movement from dependency to interdependency: from a hierarchical, controlling relationship to one based on trust, reciprocity and mutual supportive growth – any person's potential to grow, learn and develop is contingent on a social relationship. The central characteristic of any such relationship is trust, which is based in openness and in turn creates confidence in the learner. The successful learning relationship is based on trust and confidentiality which enables disclosure, challenge and questioning. Authentic relationships may be said to have the following characteristics:

- High levels of trust.
- Shared values and a commitment to mutual well-being.
- Consistency over time.
- Genuine respect, regard and affection.
- Openness, honesty and frankness.
- The ability to challenge without threat.

There is a variety of helping relationships available to support leadership development:

- Friendship: this dimension of personal and professional development is often overlooked but most successful leaders will point to a number of core, profound relationships in their lives which have been fundamental to their development.
- Counselling: highly personal and largely non-directive, designed to facilitate the emergence of understanding in the most personal aspects of personal effectiveness, growth and development.
- Mentoring: focusing on the affective dimension of professional effectiveness through supported reflection, challenge and the development and review of behavioural strategies.
- Coaching: strategies that support intervention in specific aspects of professional skills and behaviour.
- Facilitation: working collaboratively with others but with a facilitator to ensure the optimum levels of engagement and personal development.
- Training: the provision of generic skills; activities to build skills and strategies relating to particular and specific aspects of the role of leader.

For any of these learning relationships to work there needs to be a number of specific characteristics in place:

1 Challenge: not in the confrontational sense but rather asking the fundamental questions or posing problems. Challenge is fundamental to deep and profound learning and it is axiomatic to authentic personal development, according to Socrates: 'A life unexamined is not worth living'. The primary purpose of challenge is to stimulate analysis, to promote explanation and so support the achievement of understanding.

2 Feedback: this is a key strategy in all helping relationships. Its primary purpose is to provide informed, objective advice, based on evidence to support analysis of actual performance. Effective feedback needs to be specific, focused, detailed, systematic and challenging. Feedback tends to work best within an agreed agenda and as part of a developmental strategy.

3 Reflection: this is central to the development of deep and profound learning, is pivotal to successful professional practice and yet is the most elusive aspect of leadership learning. Reflection is about self-directed, structured analysis of behaviour, ideas, situations, practice or relationships and is primarily concerned with making sense of and ordering evidence or other stimuli. The purpose of reflection is to learn from experience to inform future thinking and hence action. Reflection is enhanced by support, but to be sustainable and authentic needs to be increasingly self-directed and owned. We all reflect all the time, at the end of a difficult meeting, driving home, reading the paper, at a conference when a chance comment triggers a chain of thought. However, this is often random and haphazard reflection; while valuable it does not permit sustained and fundamental questioning and analysis.

4 Developing learning strategies: one of the most important characteristics of a helping relationship is the proposing of alternative ways of working, the introduction of new ideas, suggesting different strategies and building alternative scenarios.

Authenticity is thus a product of the capacity of an individual to explore what it means to be me *and* to recognize that becoming me is, in itself, a social process. It is through social relationships that the movement to authenticity is most powerfully expressed, but this is not a passive process:

> [Leaders] . . . are proactive and seek out whatever support they need, wherever they can find it. They are so determined to learn, to change, and to shape their experiences that whatever the situation in which they find themselves they will find a way to increase the complexity of their lives. (Csikszentmihalyi, 2003, page 81)

Watkin (2000) extends this notion of complexity seeing it as richness and depth:

> We might conceptualise the person as their cluster of relationships, thinking of them as a node in a web of relationships. Similarities and differences in the features of this web (its extent, the quality of relationship, degree of connectedness and so on) turn out to make sense of many important similarities and differences between people, of the changes that may occur in their lives, and also of how change can be made in their lives. (page 70)

Watkins goes on to describe 'relational embeddedness' as being crucial to the development of any individual. Leaders need to cultivate a rich, complex and highly interactive cluster of networked relationships – the richer and more complex the range of authentic networks the more likely is effective learning and development.

In summary, leadership development is most likely to work when:

- Leaders accept responsibility for their own learning and development.
- The personal and the professional are given equal status.
- Leadership is seen in terms of values, purpose and relationships.
- Leadership development is viewed as effective learning.
- Leaders develop a rich portfolio of learning strategies.
- Effective learning is seen primarily as a social process.

10   Strategies to support transformation

This chapter offers an insight into a range of leadership strategies and techniques that may be particularly relevant in the context of transformation. The strategies are included partly to demonstrate that leadership for transformation may require very different approaches and techniques and that leadership in this context will need to include a repertoire of behaviours not normally seen as significant in this context. The strategies reviewed are:

1 storytelling
2 dialogue
3 appreciative enquiry
4 developing readiness and capability
5 using scenarios in school leadership
6 the leader as facilitator.

What these strategies have in common is that they are all concerned with the perception of relationships and reality – they do not assume objectivity but recognize the contingent nature of shared understanding.

Storytelling

Storytelling is probably as old as language itself; it is also found in every culture and every age. It is one of the most pervasive human experiences, which probably explains Gardner's 1995 contention that: 'the key to leadership is the effective communication of a story' (page 42). Denning (2005) makes an explicit link between storytelling and leading for transformation:

At a time when corporate survival often requires transformational change, leadership involves inspiring people to act in unfamiliar and often unwelcome ways. Mind-numbing cascades of numbers or daze-inducing PowerPoint slides won't achieve this goal. Even logical arguments for making the change usually won't do the trick.

But effective story telling often does. In fact in certain situations, nothing else works. (page 5)

History and culture reinforce this point: stories are found in all the great faiths – for example the parables of the Christian New Testament – they cross cultures – for example Aesop's fables and all their derivatives – and they seem to work for all ages and levels of cultural sophistication – witness the stories of the brothers Grimm. Stories make sense of the world, they create new worlds and they allow us to explore alternative realities in safety. In essence, stories convert ideas into pictures, they enrich understanding through imagery and metaphor, and there is something profoundly reassuring about a storyteller. Their role in society has long been established, venerated and attributed status and significance beyond that of narrator. Consider the experience of a one hour presentation accompanied by 45 PowerPoint slides. Compare that with a 20 minute story told with verve, rich imagery, compelling word pictures, and a degree of gusto and dramatic licence. Which is likely to be the more compelling and memorable experience? Watch people on the bus or train to see how absorbing a narrative can be as they read their novels, mercifully oblivious to the horrors of rush hour travel. In many ways and in many contexts storytelling is the most powerful way to help create shared meaning and build a common narrative that allows the development of a common language and rich, shared imagery.

For all the above reasons, Gardner's contention is almost certainly correct. If we can rethink the role of leadership in terms of narrative then we are reinforcing the essential proposition that leadership is relational and the most effective leaders are those who can best secure our engagement. In many ways the core functions of leadership: securing commitment to shared values, developing a common scenario for the future and building effective relationships can all be enriched and enhanced through the use of storytelling. Storytelling is about securing rapport and interaction:

The interactive leader comes with a message and an agenda, but also seeks to interact with the audience and learn from their viewpoints. For this purpose, storytelling is an extraordinarily suitable tool. Since all good storytelling begins and ends in listening, the session is inherently participative and interactive. (Denning, 2005, page 284)

Most of the techniques that are described in the rest of this chapter depend in varying degrees on the ability of leaders to tell stories, or to work through narrative.

The power of narrative can be explained in a number of ways:

1 It enables and encourages imagination and creativity; there are no limits to the boundaries of possibility in a story.
2 Stories make the abstract real and the complex understandable.
3 Almost all stories are person centred and this naturally secures our interest and emotional commitment. (The bad story is easily spotted – you don't care if the main characters live or die and, in the worse case, actually wish them dead.)
4 Stories allow us to explore alternative worlds vicariously and in microcosm. The characters can experience the dangers and negativity on our behalf.
5 Narrative develops its own internal logic so multiple alternative realities can be explored.
6 Narrative helps us explore the implications of change by developing a range of alternative scenarios and making them real in personal terms.
7 The language of stories enables understanding, and engages curiosity and excitement through rich imagery, narrative flow and the conventions of storytelling – 'Once upon a time'.

Think of all of the polemics written against totalitarianism – and then think of the simplicity and power of George Orwell's *Animal Farm*; the depth and strength of his critique is partly explained by the deceptively simple story line and the sense of engagement with the characters. It would be rather nice to think of school leaders starting staff meetings with 'Are you sitting comfortably? Then I'll begin.' Leaders might consider telling stories rather than sharing strategic plans; they could use stories to explore the moral basis of the school's work. They could test the feasibility of proposals for change by testing them against a range of alternative narratives. Crucially they secure the engagement and commitment of staff by telling stories of the future of the school. (See the section on scenarios later in this chapter.)

Really clever parents make bedtime stories extra special by including a character with the same name as their child – this is guaranteed to maintain interest and excitement. Wise school leaders do the same with disaffected staff – but not necessarily at bedtime.

Dialogue

It is very difficult to contemplate any process of enduring transformation that does not involve sophisticated levels of dialogue as one of the key leadership strategies and shared behaviours. Dialogue is more than effective communication; it is about relationships and enhancing the very nature of community – as George Otero expresses it:

Dialogue ... is an art and a discipline that deepens and grows more meaningful the more we engage in it. Dialogue also gets better the more we try out different moves and experiment with a variety of ways to listen more fully, speak more fluently from the heart, communicate more coherently, affirm more generously and learn more lastingly from those around us. (West-Burnham et al., 2007, page 89)

Dialogue has the same relationship to conversation as the team has to a group. In both cases there is a superficial resemblance but in reality there are fundamental differences which are to do with integrity, authenticity and effectiveness. Working in a group is usually better than working in isolation; working in a team can be exponentially more effective than working in a group. A conversation can be very powerful and is infinitely better than silence but dialogue can be transformative in terms of what is said and how it is said. Zeldin (1998), who uses conversation in the same way that I am using dialogue, points to its crucial characteristics:

Conversation is a meeting of minds with different memories and habits. When minds meet, they don't just exchange facts: they transform them, reshape them, draw different implications from them, and engage in new trains of thought. Conversation doesn't just reshuffle the cards: it creates new cards ... It's like a spark that two minds create. (page 14)

Dialogue is characterized by genuine reciprocity; it is a two way process in which there is a shared and equal commitment to respect the dignity and integrity of each of the participants. Dialogues are essentially egalitarian; leadership is contextual, informal and process orientated. Perhaps the best known dialogues in history are those written by Plato featuring the thinking of Socrates. The classic form of the Socratic dialogue is the posing of a question, the identification of a problem or the expression of a disagreement. The purpose of the dialogue is to achieve a mutually acceptable resolution by the testing of alternative hypotheses, the exclusion of inappropriate arguments and fallacious conclusions and the generation of possible solutions. A dialogue is about the achievement of shared understanding not the winning of a debate, which implies winners and losers. Modern usage of the idea of dialogue is much broader than the Socratic in the range of possible applications, it is not just a technical philosophical tool, and it is a way of collaborative working and leading.

There are countless ways in which the nature of dialogue might be understood but one way in is to think in terms of different types of dialogue which have certain characteristics in common but where the context will determine the precise nature of the dialogue. Broadly, dialogue might be understood in the following ways:

1 Personal dialogue: this is the inner dialogue that is the basis for every other dialogue. It is the reflective process, the meditation, the artistic exploration, the creative muse at work, and the personal attempts at making sense through analysing, processing and synthesizing. This is the way that we internalize issues to make sense of them. This is the inner process that enables us to make sense in the public domain. This dialogue is generated and driven by the need to make sense of and to understand self.

2 Social dialogue: this is communication in the family and between friends. This is the communication between mother and child, between those who love and are loved. It is characterized by depth, openness, frankness and directness. This dialogue is characterized by love and unconditional acceptance. It is a dialogue with a special language, with unspoken assumptions and it works through intuition as much as any explicit protocols.

3 Professional dialogue: this is the discourse of work and public interaction, the discussion between doctor and doctor; this is the master instructing the apprentice, the academics debating, the engineers problem solving. In one sense dialogue in this context is characterized by a closed 'expert' language, a specialist vocabulary – 'jargon' to the outsider. But this is also about public communication, the writer, the journalist and the professional communicator. This is also the language of leadership; the dialogue about values, the discourse on purpose, the questioning of technique and professional practice.

4 Learning dialogue: this is the process of mentoring, coaching and tutoring. It is also the language of facilitation and teaching. It is characterized by enquiry, discovery, questioning, challenge and support, nurturing, explaining and affirming. This is the relationship described by Vygotsky in his theory of the Zone of Proximal Development (see Daniels, 2001); this is scaffolding – this is Socrates at work.

5 Community dialogue: this is the process of debate, of shared decision taking. This is the telling of stories to create shared understanding of a common history. This is talk across the community on matters of shared concern, it is also gossip, acts of worship and joint celebration, and it is songs, myths and legends. It is the old initiating the young into rituals and symbols. It works through high trust, long embedded conventions, and protocols and shared understanding – as in the following description of a Native American community meeting:

> They just talked and talked and talked, apparently to no purpose. They made no decisions. There was no leader. And everybody could participate. There may have been wise men or wise women who were listened to a bit more – the older ones – but everybody could talk. The meeting went on, until it finally seemed to stop for no reason at all and the group dispersed. Yet after that, everybody seemed to know what to do, because they understood each other so well. (Bohm, 2004, pages 18, 19)

All forms of dialogue are enabled and facilitated by a range of behaviours and strategies:

- open and supportive questioning;

- respect and inclusion;
- building, extending and developing each contribution;
- analytical and synthesizing strategies and techniques are employed;
- regular feedback is used to confirm mutual comfort with content and process;
- parity of esteem between participants is assumed and reinforced;
- mutual positive affirmation and reciprocity;
- sharing anxieties and doubts;
- evidence-based review and planning;
- acceptance of silence, ambiguity and paradox;
- appreciation and celebration of outcomes and process.

Appreciative inquiry

Appreciative inquiry is a leadership and management technique that challenges the orthodox approaches to problem solving, planning and decision making in organizations. Normally the strategy adopted is essentially a deficit model approach – in essence the issues are perceived as negatives, problems to be solved and issues to be resolved. Appreciative inquiry switches the emphasis to focus on that which is known to work and be successful in the organization or the school. It is a celebration of success and an affirmation of that which is valued and felt to be of significance. This approach works on the absence of negatives – which can be challenging for many.

Appreciative inquiry can be best understood in organic terms; it enhances the potential and capacity of any living system because it acts as a positive force enhancing and building potential. The approach replaces fault finding with the discovery of success; diagnosis is replaced with dreaming; design and destiny place the emphasis on the creation of energy and the possibility of transformation. Rather than focusing on short-term incremental improvement appreciative inquiry opens the possibilities of transformation through unconditional positivity. Appreciative inquiry focuses on imagination, innovation, creativity, exploring potential and shared scenarios of preferred futures.

Figure 10.1 shows the conceptual model of appreciative inquiry and how each component of the process builds on and develops its predecessors.

The positive core is the shared understanding and celebration of that which makes the school special – what the school should be famous for. The core is identified through a shared process of celebration, recognition and appreciation.

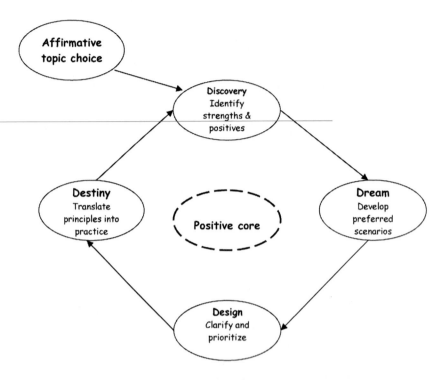

Figure 10.1 The four dimensional cycle
Source: adapted from Whitney and Trosten-Bloom, 2003, page 6

Affirmative Topic Choice
Affirmative Topics are the subjects of strategic importance to the school. They may be an aspect of the school's positive core, that if expanded would further the organization's success. They may be a problem that if stated in the affirmative and studied would improve the school's performance. Or, they may be a success factor the school needs to learn about in order to grow and change. (Whitney and Trosten-Bloom, 2003, page 7)

Discovery
This is an extensive, cooperative search to understand the 'best of what is' and 'what has been.' The Discovery process results in:

- A rich description or mapping of the organization's positive core.
- Organization-wide sharing of stories of best practices and exemplary actions.
- Enhanced organizational knowledge and collective wisdom.
- The emergence of unplanned changes well before implementation of the remaining phases of the 4-D Cycle. (pages 8–9)

Dream
An energizing exploration of 'what might be.' This phase is a time for people to collectively explore hopes and dreams for their work, their working relationships, their organisation, and the world. It is a time to envision possibilities that are big, bold, and beyond the boundaries of what has been in the past. (page 9)

Design
A set of Provocative Propositions which are statements describing the ideal organisation or 'what should be.' They expand the organisation's image of itself by presenting clear, compelling pictures of how things will be. (page 9)

Destiny
A series of inspired actions that support ongoing learning and innovation or 'what will be.' ... The Destiny phase focuses specifically on personal and organisational commitments and paths forward. In many cases, Appreciative Enquiry becomes the framework for leadership and ongoing organisational development. (page 9)

What's Distinctive about Appreciative Inquiry?
... Appreciative Inquiry is fully affirmative; by moving through the 4-D Cycle the school builds upon its track record of success and inspires positive possibilities for the future to be expressed and realized. (pages 10–11)

Appreciative inquiry is an enquiry-based process and at the heart of appreciative inquiry is the 'art of the question' – the ability to craft unconditionally positive questions. It is an approach to change with endless variation; appreciative inquiry is improvisational. It is not a singular methodology because it is not based on one firmly established way of proceeding.

Why does appreciative inquiry work?

- It builds relationships enabling people to be known in relationship, rather than in role.
- It creates an opportunity for people to be heard.
- It generates opportunities for people to dream and to share their dreams.
- It creates an environment in which people are able to choose how they contribute.
- It gives people both discretion and support to act.
- It encourages and enables people to be positive.

The components of the appreciative inquiry process are:

The positive core

- What are your organization's distinctive qualities?
- What does it do really well?

- What is worthy of celebration?
- What should we be famous for?

The affirmative topic

- What specific aspect of the organization's life do you need to focus on?
- What can be done to reinforce and extend an aspect of the organization's strengths?

Discovery

- How do our strengths work in practice?
- What does best practice actually look and feel like?
- What stories can we tell about our successes?

Dream

- How might we build on our strengths?
- How do we want to develop and grow?
- How do we want to be in the future?

Design

- What will our dreams look like in practice?
- What will the organization look like in the future?

Destiny

- What specific actions do we need to take to translate our dreams into practice?
- What are the implications of our dreams for the governance and leadership of the organization?
- What do we need to do to build sustainable capacity?

Developing readiness and capability

In the final analysis, change is a learning process – the movement from improvement to transformation is posited on a fundamental truth; organizations do not change – the people in them do. Coming to terms with the profound changes that transformation involves means that individuals have to internalize new mind maps or a new imaginary to create a new way of thinking about themselves and their organization. It would be very wrong to underestimate the challenge of transformative approaches.

Transformation, by definition, rejects much of the existing structure and prevailing norms. It will often be the case that the challenge of transformation is not so much accepting the new as being prepared to abandon the old. Change inevitably involves loss and for many people this will be an emotional (rather than rational) experience. Equally it would be wrong to assume equal levels of commitment to the proposed changes and equal aptitude and skills appropriate to working in a new context.

The potential of any individual to change, and to be effective working in the new context, can be seen as the result of a complex interaction between his or her readiness and capability:

- Readiness: the extent to which individuals are engaged, motivated, committed to the school's vision and values and are working with energy and enthusiasm.
- Capability: the levels of knowledge, skills, personal resources, experience and authority that individuals bring to the school.

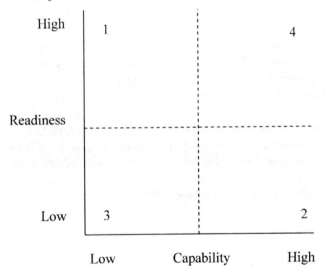

Figure 10.2 Readiness and capability
Source: adapted from Everard and Morris, 1996, page 243, in West-Burnham and Coates, 2005, page 110

Figure 10.2 demonstrates the relationship between readiness and capability, and the implications of the various permutations of the changing balance between them.

1 high readiness – low capability
   Very positive and enthusiastic but limited knowledge and expertise.

2 high capability – low readiness

Very experienced with high knowledge and skills but lacking motivation and engagement.

3 low capability – low readiness

Very limited motivation and engagement, limited skills and knowledge – no authority.

4 high capability – high readiness

Highly effective individuals with a combination of high engagement and commitment with knowledge, skills and authority.

The extent to which a school can approach any transformation strategy with confidence is directly related to the level of 'fourness'. The greater the number of staff in the top right-hand quadrant, the greater the levels of capacity, resilience and sustainability available to the school.

The model can be used to explore the potential effectiveness of a leadership team, any group or project team or the whole staff. Having located individuals on the model it is then important to move people from quadrants 1, 2 and 3. Moving people from quadrant 1 to quadrant 4 is probably the best understood strategy, as it involves mentoring and coaching. This approach is about building confidence through enhancing knowledge and experience. Moving people from quadrant 2 to quadrant 4 is more challenging. This involves what Goleman (2002) describes as 'authoritative leadership'.

Moving people from quadrant 3 may be the most challenging strategy of all. In fact it may be so challenging as to be counter-productive, in other words the levels of leadership energy required are so high that any success is essentially a Pyrrhic victory. People in this quadrant are often 'black-holes': they absorb energy and light and no interventions will work. On the other hand, from a more positive perspective, if the whole school is moving towards quadrant 4 then those in quadrant 3 will either begin to move to avoid being totally isolated or they will leave the school. Either of these options may be considered a success.

Using scenarios in school leadership

The rationale for using scenarios in leadership for transformation is to enrich leadership thinking, explore alternative perceptions of reality, and identify alternative modes of decision making when addressing important issues in the face of uncertainties. Strategic planning, in an historical sense, assumed that leadership and organizational life took place in a world that never existed; even in the most naive models of a golden age of management. The numerous alternative models of planning all assumed that the world is essentially predictable, linear and controllable – all now manifestly untrue. There is a certain comfort in developing complex and detailed plans projecting into the future; there is the reassuring illusion that there is the possibility of control. The reality is, of course, that the more extended the time frame, the more complex the variables, and the more politically significant the outcomes the less reliable is the plan. A great deal of management thinking is subject to the rationalistic fallacy – that the world is a rational place in which intentions are always translated into outcomes. The truth is rarely that simple.

The complexity of the modern world and, in particular, the complexity of the transformational process point to the need for a strategy that enables a future perspective while recognizing the problems inherent in seeking to control the future. The use of scenarios is just such an approach. Scenarios are some of the most powerful and significant stories, conversations and dialogues that we can have. At one level it is the parent and child involved in 'What will I be when I grow up?' discussion. It is lovers planning the detail of their life together in the future. It is a couple approaching retirement beginning to plan the nature and shape of their future lives. In all of these cases, what is happening is the identification, articulation and development of the components of a preferred future. All of these situations are best engaged with through narrative – building scenarios might be best seen as telling stories about the future. Just think of the prescience of the science fiction stories of Arthur C. Clarke that became science fact. In many ways he was building scenarios through narrative.

It is this same process that may be most appropriate for schools approaching transformation. Since 9/11 it has been very difficult to argue for a rational and stable world in which individuals and organizations can make assumptions with absolute confidence. Scenario-based approaches recognize the relativity and contingency of all planning processes.

Scenarios are stories: narratives that help to work out the possible options for the future by developing a range of models with varying degrees of detail and alternative possibilities. A child might switch between being a racing driver, a nurse or an explorer once working with animals has been excluded. Each of these options can then be developed and explored in terms of implications – it is the process of generating and understanding implications that gives scenario-based thinking its potential strength. The very process of building scenarios is a powerful leadership strategy serving as a means of securing engagement and creating consensus. Involvement in developing scenarios helps to secure alignment and engagement with a dream (as used in appreciative enquiry, described above). Working to identify preferred and least preferred scenarios can serve to reinforce shared values and agreement on core purpose.

There is as much art as science in developing scenarios; the process is a clear and rational one to describe, although messier to execute. In many ways the process of developing scenarios should be contingent in itself, in other words open to regular review and modification but certain generic principles and an appropriate sequence can be identified, as follows.

First, specify the major issue or decision you are facing, for instance moving towards personalizing learning or developing a community education strategy. Then focus on and explore in detail the moral framework that you wish to work in and the 'taken-for-granted' issues that have to be built in to any model of the future.

Second, isolate the key drivers – those external forces affecting your school and community. Drivers fall into two categories. There are *predetermined elements* which are relatively stable or predictable, for example demographics of the population, accountability models and policy imperatives. *Critical uncertainties* are unstable or unpredictable, for example client needs, government policies or new technologies. This stage of the process requires detailed contextual analysis and a high degree of sensitivity to environmental factors.

Third, select the two or three most important imperatives. Do not complicate scenarios by selecting too many alternative imperatives. On the basis of the chosen imperatives, start the process of formulating three or four scenarios with contrasting futures: (1) the baseline, how will the future be if nothing really changes scenario; (2) the scenario in which imperative A alone dominates; (3) the scenario in which imperative B alone dominates; and (4) perhaps one with various permutations explored.

Fourth, create a short internally consistent story of the future that highlights the key implications of the imperatives or drivers for each scenario. The story should develop in detail the most significant variables and explore the practical implications and alternative ways forward. Thus, in personal terms, a person may develop a range of preferred career scenarios all of which are an expression of personal ambition and a desire to be an effective and successful educator – the alternatives might involve different timescales to headship, working in different types of schools, or moving into administration. These in turn might be modified by a partner's career plans, the needs of children and so on.

Fifth, identify the optimum scenario in terms of moral purpose, pragmatic decisions, preferred futures and external imperatives. Identify the least preferred scenario. This process may be facilitated by the identification of a range of criteria that specifies the acceptable boundaries for decision making or the 'no-go' areas. Review the possible implications of the preferred and least preferred scenarios. Is this what you actually want? It is sometimes the case that a dream scenario becomes a nightmare when the practical implications are fully understood.

Sixth, select indicators, success criteria or performance measures which will allow analysis of how a particular scenario is emerging. Choose those factors that will initiate and inform action when a particular threshold is reached. Identify strategies to track and review these indicators regularly and then modify and update the scenarios appropriately.

One of the key strengths of the scenario planning approach is that it is an iterative strategy. The process is organic and dynamic, growing, modifying and building the scenarios in response to an emerging future.

Finally, usually at some future date, make those decisions that are appropriate for the particular future that does unfold. Future reality, of course, is unlikely to be exactly in accord with any of your scenarios, but the flexible mindset developed during scenario planning enables you to respond appropriately to events that do occur. You do not choose among the scenarios. Rather, you use them all to help form hypotheses about the world and recognize which ones are operative at any given time – assuming that there is consistency and congruity with the school's core purpose and moral integrity.

The leader as facilitator

Effective facilitation is one of the great social arts; at its best it represents an astonishing blend of interpersonal skills, political sensitivity and professional knowledge. At its most basic, facilitation is a process by which a group is enabled to work more effectively by an individual who may not necessarily have positional status or authority in the group. A facilitator's authority comes from possessing skills, strategies and behaviours that support a group in achieving its aims or goals. Thus individual leaders with positional status may find that the most effective leadership behaviour they can employ is to empower a colleague by asking him or her to facilitate.

The facilitator works by ensuring the optimum effectiveness of each member of the group – a classic example of 'the whole being more than the sum of the parts'. This involves a commitment to each group member's rights to inclusion and participation, working in good faith and creating a culture of trust, respect and reciprocity. One of the most important contributions of the facilitator is to ensure that the personal dignity of each participant is respected and his or her identity is valued and honoured. It is equally important that the facilitator creates a sense of ownership by the group of the outcomes – if not invisible leadership then certainly very low profile.

There is a very real issue around how far the facilitator should be neutral. Certainly the facilitator does not use his or her position to advance his or her own ideas or beliefs – that is totally inappropriate. At the same time it is very important that the facilitator is not totally disempowered, especially if a group is struggling. It might be best expressed as the facilitator is content neutral but process committed. Equally the facilitator does not have to indulge or ignore inappropriate language or behaviours by group members or morally unacceptable statements. The range of options for a facilitator is exemplified in the models shown in Figure 10.3, which demonstrate the wide number of permutations available.

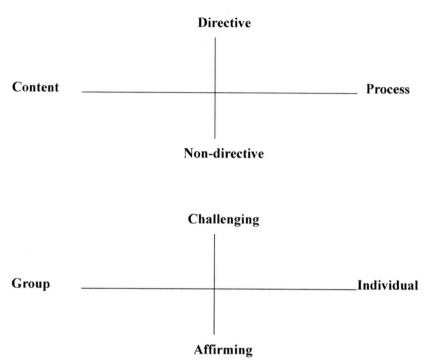

Figure 10.3 Options for effective facilitation
Source: Collarbone and West-Burnham, 2008, page 57

The optimum position in each part of Figure 10.3 will depend on the level of maturity of the group, the status and significance of the particular process being facilitated and the willingness of the group to be guided. The ability of a facilitator to work in a totally non-directive way and only work through affirmation is entirely contingent on the sophistication of the group. In an ideal world, and assuming relatively sophisticated groups, one might look for:

- non-direction on content but explicit direction on process;
- challenge for the group and affirmation for the individual.

Equally one would hope that school leaders would work to build capacity in group work so that the need for direction diminishes. Facilitation by school leaders is a classic example of modelling appropriate behaviours as it could be argued that facilitation is a very powerful strategy to support student learning, although in direct contradistinction to much classroom practice. I suspect that staff meetings and in-service sessions that are facilitated will be more effective than those that are 'managed'. Equally the idea of the teacher as facilitator coincides with what we understand about enabling effective learning, the importance of scaffolding learning and developing high quality relationships in the learning environment.

There can be no exhaustive list of the activities that facilitators engage in but the following are indicative of the core elements of the role:

- Clarifying, articulating and securing agreement about the purpose of the event.
- Confirming membership, roles and relationships.
- Maintaining a focus on the key task and managing time.
- Establishing working protocols and securing adherence to them.
- Using techniques to assist problem solving and consensus building.
- Asking open questions that encourage participation.
- Giving feedback through paraphrasing to confirm understanding.
- Summarizing and synthesizing to encourage the discussion to move forward.
- Proposing solutions and formulations to break deadlocks.
- Testing understanding across the group.
- Creating safe spaces for reluctant participants.
- Managing the exuberant verbosity of some participants.
- Ensuring that the group recognizes, appreciates and celebrates contributions.
- Insisting on monitoring and review to inform future meetings.

The effective facilitator is a paragon of virtue. While much of the above can be developed through training and reflection on experience over time there is little doubt that there are also facilitation qualities which may not be directly amenable to training; they are best seen as personal dispositions which may not be related to role, age or status – thus the most effective facilitator may not necessarily be the most senior or experienced person present. What is clear is that the effective facilitator works consistently to model a range of appropriate and valid behaviours and works to avoid other behaviours.

A list of the qualities of effective facilitators is shown in Table 10.1.

Table 10.1 The qualities of effective facilitators

Do	Do not
Create energy	Patronize/condescend
Show flexibility	Use sarcasm
Allow silence	Be negative
Encourage reflection	Be didactic
Value people	Take sides
Display enthusiasm	Abuse their role
Share leadership	Offer opinions
Make assumptions explicit	Indulge groupthink
Model courtesy	Accept false consensus

Conclusion

However effective these techniques, there is nothing as compelling as morally confident, personally authentic leadership which displays the most powerful qualities of all: energy, excitement, enthusiasm and enjoyment – it is difficult to see how transformation will be achieved except through leaders who display these most significant but most elusive and fragile qualities.

References

Apple, M.W. (1982) *Education and Power*, ARK Edition, London: Routledge & Kegan Paul

Atwater, L.E. and Atwater, D.C. (1994) 'Organizational Transformation: Strategies for Change and Improvement', in Bass, B.M. and Avolio, B.J. (eds) *Improving Organizational Effectiveness Through Transformational Leadership*, London: Sage

Bass, B.M. and Avolio, B.J. (1994) *Improving Organizational Effectiveness Through Transformational Leadership*, London: Sage

Beare, H. (2001) *Creating the Future School*, London: RoutledgeFalmer

Bennis, W. (1989) *On Becoming a Leader*, London: Century Business

Bennis, W. and Goldsmith, J. (1997) *Learning to Lead*, London: Nicholas Brealey Publishing

Black, J.S. and Gregersen, H.B. (2002) *Leading Strategic Change*, Upper Saddle River, NJ: Prentice Hall

Bohm, D. (2004) *On Dialogue*, Abingdon: Routledge

Boisvert, R.D. (1998) *John Dewey Rethinking Our Time*, Albany, NY: State University of New York Press

Bryk, A.S. and Schneider, B. (2002) *Trust in Schools*, New York: Russell Sage

Caine, R.N. and Caine, G. (1997) *Education on the Edge of Possibility*, Alexandria, VA: ASCD

Capra, F. (2002) *The Hidden Connections*, London: HarperCollins

Chomsky, N. (2000) *Chomsky on Miseducation*, Lanham, MD: Rowman & Littlefield

Collarbone, P. and West-Burnham, J. (2008) *Understanding Systems Leadership: Securing Excellence and Equity in Education*, London: Network Continuum

Collini, S. (2006) *Absent Minds*, Oxford: Oxford University Press

Covey, S.M.R. (2006) *The Speed of Trust*, London: Simon and Schuster

Crick, B. (2002) *Democracy: A Very Short Introduction*, Oxford: Oxford University Press

Csikszentmihalyi, M. (1997) *Finding Flow*, New York: Basic Books

Csikszentmihalyi, M. (2003) *Good Business*, New York: Viking

Cummings, T. and Keen, J. (2008) *Leadership Landscapes*, Basingstoke: Palgrave Macmillan

Damasio, A. (2003) *Looking for Spinoza*, London: Heinemann

Daniels, H. (2001) *Vygotsky & Pedagogy*, London: RoutledgeFalmer

Dantley, M.E. and Tillman, L.C. (2006) 'Social Justice and Moral Transformative Leadership', in Marshall, C. and Oliva, M. (eds) *Leadership for Social Justice*, Boston, MA: Pearson Education

De Geus, A. (1997) *The Living Company*, London: Nicholas Brealey Publishing

Dennett, D. (2006) *Breaking the Spell*, London: Penguin Allen Lane

Denning, S. (2005) *The Leaders Guide to Storytelling*, San Francisco, CA: Jossey-Bass

Department for Children, Schools and Families (DCSF) (2007) *The Children's Plan*, London: DCSF

Department for Education and Skills (DfES) (2002) *Leadership Incentive Grant: Guidance*, www.standards.dfes.gov.uk/school improvement/

Department for Education and Skills (DfES) (2004) *A National Conversation about Personalised Learning*, London: DfES, www.standards.dfes.gov.uk/personalised learning/downloads/personalisedlearning.pdf

Dewey, J. (1933) *How We Think*, Boston, MA: Houghton Mifflin Company

Diamond, J. (2005) *Collapse*, London: Allen Lane

Duignan, P. (2006) Educational Leadership: Key Challenges and Ethical Tensions, Cambridge: Cambridge University Press

Ehrenreich, B. (2007) *Dancing in the Streets*, London: Granta Books

Everard, K.B. and Morris, G. (1996) *Effective School Management*, London: Paul Chapman Publishing

Flintham, A. (2008) '"Reservoirs of Hope": Sustaining Passion in Leadership', in Davies, B. and Brighouse, T. (eds) *Passionate Leadership in Education*, London: Sage

Forgacs, D. (ed.) (1999) *The Antonio Gramsci Reader*, London: Lawrence & Wishart

Freire, P. (1992) *Pedagogy of Hope*, London: Continuum

Fullan, M. (2001) *Leading in a Culture of Change*, San Francisco, CA: Jossey-Bass

Fullan, M. (2003) *The Moral Imperative of School Leadership*, Thousand Oaks, CA: Corwin Press

Furedi, F. (2003) 'Room for Debate?', *Guardian Education Supplement*, 17 June

Furedi, F. (2004) *Where Have All the Intellectuals Gone?*, London: Continuum

Gardner, H. (1995) *Leading Minds*, New York: Basic Books

Gardner, H. (1999) *The Disciplined Mind*, New York: Simon and Schuster

Gardner, H. (2004) *Changing Minds*, Boston, MA: Harvard Business School Publishing

Gardner, H. (2006) *The Development and Education of the Mind*, Abingdon: Routledge

Gardner, H., Csikszentmihalyi, M. and Damon, W. (2001) *Good Work*, New York: Basic Books

Giroux, H.A. (1997) *Pedagogy and the Politics of Hope*, New York: Westview Press

Gladwell, M. (2000) *The Tipping Point*, London: Abacus

Gloor, P.A. (2006) *Swarm Creativity*, Oxford: Oxford University Press

Goleman, D. (1998) *Emotional Intelligence*, New York: Bantam Books

Goleman, D. (2002) *The New Leaders*, London: Little Brown

Goleman, D. (2006) *Social Intelligence*, London: Hutchinson

Grafen, A. and Ridley, M. (eds) (2006) *Richard Dawkins: How a Scientist Changed the Way we Think*, Oxford: Oxford University Press

Guignon, C. (2004) *On Being Authentic*, London: Routledge

Handy, C. (1994) *The Empty Raincoat*, London: BCA

Hargreaves, D.H. (2003) *Education Epidemic*, London: DEMOS

Hargreaves, D.H. (2004) Personalising Learning, London: Specialist Schools Trust

Heifetz, R.A. (2003) 'Adaptive Work', in Bentley, T. and Wilsdon, J. (eds) *The Adaptive State*, London: DEMOS

Hock, D. (1999) *Birth of the Chaordic Age*, San Francisco, CA: Berrett-Keohler

Holland, J.H. (1998) *Emergence from Chaos to Order*, Oxford: Oxford University Press

Homer-Dixon, T. (2000) *The Ingenuity Gap*, London: Jonathan Cape

Istance, D. (2002) *Schooling for the Future: Trends, Scenarios and Lifelong Learning*, paper presented at the International Seminar on Educational Infrastructure, Guadalajara, Mexico, 24–27 February

Johnson, P. (1988) *Intellectuals*, New York: Harper & Row

Johnson, S. (2001) *Emergence*, London: The Penguin Press

Judt, T. (2001) 'Introduction', in Camus, A. *The Plague*, London: Modern Penguin Classics

Judt, T. (2008) *Reappraisals*, New York: The Penguin Press

Kelley, T. (2005) *The Ten Faces of Innovation*, New York: Doubleday

Kuhn, T.S. (1970) *The Structure of Scientific Revolutions*, Chicago, IL: The University of Chicago Press

Lambert, L. (1998) *Building Leadership Capacity in Schools*, Alexandria, VA: ASCD

Leadbeater, C. (2008) *We-Think*, London: Profile Books

Lévy, B.-H. (ed.) (2000) *What Good Are Intellectuals?*, New York: Alogra Publishing

Marshall, S.P. (1995) www.21learn.org/publ/systhesis/synthesis_four.htm

Martin, R. and Barresi, J. (2006) *The Rise and Fall of Soul and Self*, New York: Columbia University Press

Monbiot, G. (2003) *The Age of Consent*, London: Harper Perennial

Nussbaum, M. (1997) *Cultivating Humanity*, Cambridge, MA: Harvard University Press

O'Donohue, J. (1997) *Anam Cara*, London: Bantam Books

O'Malley, J.W. (2004) *Four Cultures of the West*, Cambridge, MA: Belknap Press

O'Sullivan, E. (1999) *Transforming Learning: Educational Vision for the 21st Century*, London: Zed Books

OECD (2001) *What Schools for the Future?*, Paris: OECD

Otero, G. (2001) *RelationaLearning*, Cheltenham, Australia: Hawker Brownlow

Patey, R. (2004a) *Learners as Leaders*, Coventry: HTI

Patey, R. (2004b) The BT Schools Awareness Supplement, *Guardian*, 21 September

Perkins, D. (1981) *The Mind's Best Work*, Cambridge, MA: Harvard University Press

Pont, B., Nusche, D. and Hopkins, D. (2008) *Improving School Leadership: Volume 2. Case Studies on System Leadership*, Paris: OECD

Preskill, S., Vermilya, L. and Otero, G. (2000) *Skills for Democracy*, Victoria, Australia: Hawker Brownlow Education

Putnam, R.D. and Feldstein, L.M. (2003) *Better Together*, New York: Simon & Schuster

Said, E.W. (1994) *Representations of the Intellectual*, New York: Vintage

Senge, P., Scharmer, C.O., Jaworski, J. and Flowers, B.S. (2004) *Presence*, Cambridge, MA: SoL

Sennett, R. (2008) *The Craftsman*, London: Allen Lane

Sergiovanni, T. (1992) *Moral Leadership: Getting to the Heart of School Improvement*, San Francisco, CA: Jossey-Bass

Sergiovanni, T. (2005) *Strengthening the Heartbeat*, San Francisco, CA: Jossey-Bass

Singer, P. (1997) *How Are We to Live?*, Oxford: OPUS

Solomon, R.C. (2002) *Spirituality for the Skeptic*, New York: Oxford University Press

Stein, S. and Book, H. (2000) *The EQ Edge*, Toronto: Stoddart

Steiner, G. (2003) *Lessons of the Masters*, Cambridge, MA: Harvard University Press

Sternberg, R.J. (1990) *Wisdom*, Cambridge: Cambridge University Press

Sternberg, R.J. (2005) 'A Model of Educational Leadership: Wisdom, Intelligence and Creativity Synthesized', *International Journal of Leadership in Education*, Vol. 8, No. 4, October–December, 347–364

Sunstein, C. (2006) *Infotopia*, New York: Oxford University Press

Surowiecki, J. (2004) *The Wisdom of Crowds*, London: Little Brown

Taffinder, P. (1998) *Big Change*, Chichester: John Wiley

Tapscott, D. and Williams, A.D. (2006) *Wikinomics*, London: Atlantic Books

Taylor, C. (1991) *The Ethics of Authenticity*, London: Harvard University Press

Taylor, C. (2004) *Modern Social Imaginaries*, Durham, NC: Duke University Press

Times Educational Supplement (TES) (2003) '2020 Vision Supplement', *Times Educational Supplement*, 24 January

Toffler, A. (1981) *The Third Wave*, London: Pan Books

Uglow, J. (2002) *The Lunar Men*, London: Faber and Faber

Vernon, M. (2005) *Wellbeing*, Stocksfield: Acumen

Watkin, C. (2000) 'The Leadership Program for Serving Headteachers: Probably the World's Largest Leadership Development Initiative', *Leadership and Organization Development Journal*, Vol. 2, No. 1, 13–19

Wenger, E. (1998) *Communities of Practice*, Cambridge: Cambridge University Press

West-Burnham, J. (2007) *Leadership Development and Personal Effectiveness*, Nottingham: NCSL

West-Burnham, J. and Coates, M. (2005) *Personalizing Learning: Transforming Education for Every Child*, London: Network Educational Press

West-Burnham, J., Farrar, M. and Otero, G. (2007) *Schools and Communities: Working Together to Transform Children's Lives*, London: Network Continuum

Wheen, F. (2004) *How Mumbo-Jumbo Conquered the World*, London: Fourth Estate

Whitney, D. and Trosten-Bloom, A. (2003) *The Power of Appreciative Inquiry*, San Francisco, CA: Barrett-Koehler Publishers

Woods, G. (2007) 'The "Bigger Feeling", The Importance of Spiritual Leadership in Educational Leadership', *Educational Management Administration and Leadership*, Vol. 35, No. 1, January, 135–160

Zeldin, T. (1998) *Conversation*, London: The Harvill Press

Zorn, D. and Boler, M. (2007) 'Rethinking Emotions and Educational Leadership', *International Journal of Leadership in Education*, Vol. 10, No. 2, April–June, 137–151

Index

Diagrams and tables are given in italics.